Succeeding as an English Teacher

ABIGAIL MANN, LYNDSAY BAWDEN, FE BREWER, DAVINA CANHAM, MARY HIND-PORTLEY, RUTH HOLDER, KALEY MACIS-RILEY, LAURA MAY ROWLANDS, ANDY SAMMONS, ZARA SHAH, LAURA TSABET AND HOLLY WIMBUSH

BLOOMSBURY EDUCATION

LONDON   OXFORD   NEW YORK   NEW DELHI   SYDNEY

BLOOMSBURY EDUCATION
Bloomsbury Publishing Plc
50 Bedford Square, London, WC1B 3DP, UK
29 Earlsfort Terrace, Dublin 2, Ireland

BLOOMSBURY, BLOOMSBURY EDUCATION and the Diana logo are
trademarks of Bloomsbury Publishing Plc

First published in Great Britain, 2021

A catalogue record for this book is available from the British Library

ISBN: PB: 978-1-4729-8941-3; ePDF: 978-1-4729-8940-6;
ePub: 978-1-4729-8942-0

2 4 6 8 10 9 7 5 3 1 (paperback)

Typeset by Newgen KnowledgeWorks Pvt. Ltd., Chennai, India
Printed and bound in the UK by CPI Group Ltd, CR0 4YY

To find out more about our authors and books visit www.bloomsbury.com
and sign up for our newsletters

Contents

Foreword v

Introduction 1

1 Early career teacher success 5
Laura Tsabet, Fe Brewer and Andy Sammons

2 Subject knowledge 29
Laura May Rowlands, Davina Canham and Holly Wimbush

3 Planning and assessment 51
Kaley Macis-Riley, Laura May Rowlands, Lyndsay Bawden and Mary Hind-Portley

4 The importance of literature 79
Mary Hind-Portley and Fe Brewer

5 Writing in English 101
Laura Tsabet, Holly Wimbush, Abigail Mann, Zara Shah, Davina Canham and Laura May Rowlands

6 Reading in English 127
Mary Hind-Portley, Kaley Macis-Riley, Lyndsay Bawden, Davina Canham and Fe Brewer

7 Vocabulary 155
Lyndsay Bawden, Abigail Mann and Fe Brewer

8 The science of learning 171
Zara Shah and Abigail Mann

9   Revision 199
       Abigail Mann and Laura May Rowlands

10 Becoming a head of department 213
        Ruth Holder and Andy Sammons

References 236
Index 242
Authors' biographies 247

Foreword

This is the book I wish I'd had when I embarked on a career as a teacher of English in 1980. It's unfortunate that so few of the authors were born at the time…

It is a comprehensive, practical and balanced guide which covers the early days of English teaching, the wide-ranging elements of the English teacher's role, and preparation for moving to lead an English department, should that be the path you decide to pursue. It is a collaborative tour de force: as the authors say in the Introduction, it is 'a testament to the collegiate approach we value so much in teaching'. The book is impressively referenced and robustly research-informed, encouraging the reader to relate its advice to their own specific context and apply the learning intentionally and thoughtfully. Case studies exemplify and strengthen underpinning principles and flesh out advice by showing its application. This is a joyful and celebratory exploration of a role which all the authors clearly relish, and their energy, enthusiasm and commitment are evident throughout as they share their insights.

These insights include the following:

- the importance of forming the most positive relationships with our colleagues, as well as with the pupils we teach;

- how we can find a manageable, sustainable balance in our lives so that we function effectively and avoid burn-out;

- the primacy of subject-knowledge and how we can develop it securely and with building confidence;

- a brilliant, wide-ranging list of resources which should transform any English teacher's professional life;

- an exploration of the fundamental purpose of assessment, and what we can do to ensure it is as effective as it can possibly be;

- discussion of the best way to go about designing a curriculum in English;

- an examination of the power of story, and a consideration of seminal texts across the ages and across the world;

- how we might best teach writing, reading, the knowledge and confident use of vocabulary, and the most successful revision strategies in English;

- and how an understanding and appreciation of the science of learning can strengthen our teaching of English

The book is also a tribute to the power of Twitter, which brought these professionals together in such a purposeful, productive and successful way – an undertaking from which future generations of English teachers will certainly benefit.

Thank you all!

Jill Berry, former English teacher, former head and now a leadership development consultant
August 2021

Introduction

This book isn't just another book about teaching. We believe it is the first of its kind. When we wrote this book, we wanted it to be useful for any English teacher, at any time in their career. We believe it does just that. It has been designed to take the English teacher on a journey, from those exciting and exhausting first few years as a newly qualified English teacher, all the way through to the dizzying and daunting heights of leadership, and fronting your very own English team. In the chapters that follow, you will find an answer for almost every question you may have as an English teacher. This book was such a joy to write and is a testament to the collegiate approach we value so much in teaching. Each of the twelve authors turned friends, located across the breadth of the UK, is rightly proud of what we have achieved. It represents hours of wonderful discussion, planning and writing, culminating in this much-needed guide.

The book takes you on a journey through the labyrinth that is English teaching, with each chapter being a new turning point towards success. You'll likely begin your journey with *Chapter 1: Early career teacher success*. As you navigate this pathway, you'll come across an abundance of ideas, from how to thrive in year one, behaviour management and making the most of feedback, to finding the signpost to your next endeavour. It is worth noting here that this chapter contains relevant information for a teacher at any stage of their career; it serves as a reminder to regularly reinforce and review your practice. As you become more settled with your route through, you'll enter the realm of *Chapter 2: Subject knowledge*, where you will discover a wealth of information about both how important subject knowledge is and how to develop it. Parallel to this realm is *Chapter 3: Planning and assessment*, where a discussion will be had, and thinking will be prompted in terms of your attitude towards curriculum design, powerful knowledge and the meaning of assessment itself. Moving forward, you'll walk through *Chapter 4: The importance of literature*, a garden of literary movements through time, and how they have opened and continue to open eyes, and broaden minds for all. As you leave with the passion for your subject reignited by the literary garden, you have a choice of routes: *Chapter 5: Writing in English*, *Chapter 6: Reading in English* and *Chapter 7: Vocabulary*. While each route is vitally important in creating well-crafted English learners, the journey through each is your decision to make and you'll leave with a plethora of practical, research-informed ideas to take forward into your own context and to carry along the way of your journey as a successful English teacher.

Chapter 8: The science of learning, the brain of the labyrinth, is where you will explore metacognition, the working memory and strategies such as retrieval practice. Whilst here, you might find it useful to track back to *Chapter 3: Planning and assessment*, as this chapter will support you to plan and assess effectively, so that everything that you do is underpinned with the principles of cognitive science.

Now it is time to begin your way out of the labyrinth through the corridor that is *Chapter 9: Revision*. Here you'll find a handful of fruitful revision strategies to use alongside all the other experiences you've had along this journey.

You have now traversed this maze and accumulated the distance that you need to succeed as an English teacher. Nobody is saying that this is all the learning that you need to do, as we are all constantly developing. Perhaps you'll choose a different realm to that of head of department for your future career path, but the final step as you leave the labyrinth is *Chapter 10: Becoming a head of department*. Here, you'll gain insights from experienced leaders of English, ranging from securing that role and building a team, to developing that team. Whether you decide that curriculum leadership is for you, it's a valuable chapter in developing leadership strategies nonetheless.

Congratulations! You've navigated the labyrinth that is *Succeeding as an English Teacher* and you can now press ahead in your own journey, taking and adapting what you have learnt into your own contexts. Our journey started where you are now, and it led to this: originally a group of teachers who met via Twitter, now a group of friends and co-authors who write all about English teaching, and continue to learn and develop from each other and all those around them, both at work and online.

We hope you enjoy this book as much as we have enjoyed writing it for you.

1

Early career teacher success

Laura Tsabet, Fe Brewer and Andy Sammons

Introduction

There are a number of texts and blogs out there about 'surviving' your first year of teaching, as though this year is a year to be endured and not enjoyed. We refute this. You've passed your training and achieved your qualified teacher status (QTS). That is something to be wholeheartedly celebrated and this year should be an opportunity for you to enjoy the benefits of your QTS: your own classroom; your own tutor group; your own classes; and the opportunity to experiment (largely unjudged) with a variety of teaching strategies until you settle on what works best for you and your pupils. It's wonderful being an early career teacher (ECT). This chapter seeks to celebrate this wonderfulness, whilst also acknowledging the challenges you may face, potential pitfalls and stumbling blocks that might attempt to throw you off course, and the things that you can hopefully do to make these challenging years slightly less challenging. It's likely to be a chapter of contradictions, but isn't that the beauty of teaching and schools? Contradictions are everywhere and we must embrace them.

Research and theory

The NFER's 2020 'Teacher labour market' report described how the 'retention rate of newly qualified teachers (NQTs) into their second year of teaching has continued to fall, as has the rate for second years going into their third year'. This is obviously not ideal; teacher-training application rates have increased but so have teacher shortages over the last five years. With many ECTs leaving the profession between their first and second years of teaching, it seems we have quite a problem. The good news is that the Early Career Framework (ECF) roll-out later this year, and the increase in teachers' starting salaries, will hopefully help to make those challenging first years in the profession more manageable and improve retention for ECTs.

The Department for Education's ITT Core Content Framework and the ECF commit to providing a structured programme for trainees and ECTs in their first three years in the profession. The aim of the programme is to give these teachers the tools and support they will need for this duration, hopefully reducing the numbers of them leaving the profession in the five years after qualifying. Although this programme is not dissimilar to the previous NQT induction period, these new frameworks are a welcome change from the policies of old. Under the new framework, the Department for Education has committed to creating free training materials, guaranteeing reductions in timetables for the two years following initial teacher training, funding time for mentors to support ECTs and also funding for mentor training.

There is a clear difference too though, in that this new framework, which has been independently reviewed by the Education Endowment Foundation (EEF), is underpinned by the 'best available research evidence' and 'expert guidance'.

This is something that we should embrace; never before has government policy concerning teacher training been so clear in its assertion that training should be backed by research. This could be the start of something wonderful. In five years, it could be normal practice for all teachers in all schools to be well versed in the science of how students learn and the impact that this has on chosen teaching strategies. Moreover, it could necessitate a move to more of a shared dialogue or common language when talking about teaching and learning.

While you work alongside a range of experienced and expert teachers, you may find at times that you wonder how on earth they do what they do with such ease; you may even envy them this and wonder if you'll ever be so adept. Here it is worth acknowledging that teachers (along with all other adults) operate differently depending on their experience and stage of expertise, and as a 'novice' (that is a new, relatively inexperienced) teacher, you will inevitably operate in a different way to experienced teachers.

The 'novice' stage of teaching (as per the Dreyfus model, which is widely used to describe stages of adult skill acquisition) is characterised by a number of behaviours which you may identify with: trying other people's ideas, explicit and detailed planning, and a desire to follow lesson 'rules' and strategies, which can offer comfort and structure. As educational psychologists Borko et al. (1990) state, 'For novices to take off in their teaching airplane, so to speak, without crashing, this requires considerable preparation.'

According to education lecturer Dr Linda Enow and education professor Andrew Goodwyn (2017), one of the most noticeable aspects of being a novice teacher is that you'll probably find that your planning processes are 'very visible' in comparison to those of more experienced teachers. You may also find that while your colleagues use few resources and adapt their lessons effortlessly in response to students' needs, you find comfort in slideshows and set lesson structures and 'rules', which provide direction for your lessons. You may also find that you feel more tired than your colleagues, as while their decision-making processes are automatic, yours are cognitively taxing as you find yourself constantly having to construct ways of responding to new situations.

While this can all seem rather negative and daunting, it is important to remember that *all* teachers began as novices, and it is a very necessary stage. As Enow and Goodwyn (2018) put it, 'Inevitably, all English teachers begin at a novice stage and this term "novice" is important to be seen not as a problem but as *an entitlement.*'

In short, you are unlikely to plan and teach as easily as your colleagues, but the planning, reading and thinking you do in your ECT years are important processes; no one becomes an expert without first being a novice.

Putting it into practice

Thriving in year one: building support networks

One of the most important, but often overlooked, aspects of thriving as a teacher is building strong relationships with colleagues. As teachers, we spend a huge amount of time with the young people in our care, but it is those relationships we have with our team that help us survive and thrive. The Department for Education is keen to recognise this too: within the ITT Core Content Framework, the word 'expert' appears 107 times, clearly drawing the need for new teachers to work with others in order to benefit from their experience and expertise. This is continued into the ECF where the phrase 'and additional guidance from expert practitioners' appears in each strand.

It is easy, however, to get caught up in Part One of the Teachers' Standards, which involves work with pupils, but during those important two years spent as an ECT, it's important to consider the meaning and importance of Part Two ('Personal and Professional Conduct') because it's personal and professional relationships with the team around you that can make or break a teacher's career.

Your immediate teaching team

The first round of people you'll need good relationships with are the team you immediately work with; often this will be your department. The easy way in here is a shared love of English: reading novels, going to the theatre, enjoying poetry or appreciating art, history or film, which forms the hinterland of our subject. But professional relationships are much more than this. They are built on shared purpose, shared values and mutual respect. Your relationship with different team members is likely to vary depending on a number of factors: which colleagues you share classes with, if you share a classroom or workspace with anyone, and your perspectives on education and young people.

Where you share classes, regular communication is key: it's easy for both parties to feel they are doing the most, or indeed, to feel they needn't do as much as the other. Fundamentally, shared classes are shared responsibility and both parties need to communicate with clarity so the pupils experience consistent language, expectations and standards. As a new teacher, this may mean that you agree to edit the terminology you use, or the approaches you take, but don't feel that sharing a class means you have to abandon these: collaboration and negotiation are important here too.

If you share a working space or classroom with others, setting ground rules or expectations can be valuable. Some teachers are more than happy to work surrounded by stacks of paper, pens and books; others like an uncluttered and organised space. Establishing some clear expectations, such as cleaning whiteboards after lessons and ensuring the computer is logged off, may seem trivial, but they can have a significant impact on others' lessons; enabling others to work shows respect for them both personally and professionally.

Academic and pastoral colleagues

Teachers don't operate solely in departments; pastoral teams, the special educational needs and disabilities (SEND) team and teaching assistants (TAs) are all part of the vehicle that enables teaching and learning to happen. Building relationships with these people can make tricky situations with students or parents a whole lot easier. TAs and pastoral teams can offer invaluable insight as to students' home lives and how they are performing in other subjects, so don't be afraid to contact them for advice, no matter how silly you might think your question or query is. Sending a quick email to forewarn them and being ready to offer concrete examples (for example, notes of things a pupil has said in class, or examples from an exercise book) will show that you've considered things in advance and that you respect them offering their time.

Pastoral teams will often have various charity fundraisers, house events and assemblies to run (among many other things), so if you've a spare moment, volunteering to lend a hand is another good way of building stronger relationships while also gaining experience. As an English specialist, you have lots to offer in regards to literacy and reading, and while these are absolutely not the exclusive responsibility of English teachers, sharing your knowledge and enthusiasm will be invaluable to many.

The wider team

Schools are kept going not by the teachers, but by a wide range of non-teaching staff: administrators, IT support, premises, reprographics, HR and so many more. When you're focused on teaching, it's easy to forget that, when you're in a pickle, these are likely to be the people who save your bacon! Don't underestimate the important role all of these people play. They deserve our respect as much as the senior leadership team (SLT) and it costs nothing to be friendly, thankful and courteous: manners go a long way.

What to expect from your mentor

The ITT Core Content Framework states that ECTs should receive 'clear, consistent and effective mentoring' as part of their multi-year entitlement. What this means is that your school's SLT must identify and appoint a mentor for you who has the knowledge and necessary skills to provide effective coaching and guidance on planning, teaching, assessment and professional standards.

With the ECF also promising funding for time with mentors and making providers and schools accountable for meeting these requirements, this means that your mentor must be given dedicated *protected* time away from the classroom to support you throughout the programme. With English being a core subject, some schools can be reluctant to allow great English teachers additional time off-timetable, so it is vital that mentors check their allocations and request for ECT meetings to be protected on their timetable from day one.

Your mentor will have been selected because they are a highly skilled member of the team and an excellent role model. Their job is to share with you their passion for the subject and the vast wealth of knowledge that they have accumulated over their career thus far, whilst simultaneously providing you with the tools and guidance that you need to be successful inside *and* outside the classroom for your first years of teaching and beyond. You should expect to receive feedback on a regular basis – not just from pre-arranged formal lesson observations, but from informal drop-ins, co-planning and professional dialogues. This is their moral obligation as your mentor and it is important to flag it up in a hurry if you are not receiving this level of support.

Any self-reflective practitioner will recognise that they are not the fountain of all knowledge, nor the guru of all teaching strategies; we all have our Achilles' heel, whether it's live modelling story-writing, teaching Chaucer, explaining auxiliary verbs, or spotting allusions to Greek mythology. Your mentor should therefore be able to direct you to observe a number of staff across the English department who can support you in your areas for subject development (as well as across the school for general pedagogy, pastoral or behavioural development), giving you the opportunity to learn different things from different people. By finding experienced voices, perhaps collating a number of mini-mentors for yourself across the school, you will be more likely to flourish. Schools are fundamentally places of learning and relationships, and your growth depends on being exposed to a variety of practitioners.

You may find that there are occasionally contrasting messages from your English mentor and your professional mentor. This can be problematic and confusing. If this is the case, it is best to be open and honest with your mentor about where you see their feedback is at odds with the professional mentor's. Your mentor's role is to ensure that your professional development needs are catered for; they should be able to put your mind at ease. It could be that your professional mentor is thinking holistically, whereas your English mentor is thinking about how they would be teaching the subject, or perhaps they're saying the same thing in different ways. If the school lacks a common language for talking about teaching and learning, then this could be the case.

How to save time

As a first-year ECT, you are entitled to a ten per cent reduction in timetable to that of more experienced colleagues (five per cent in your second year). You're expected to use this time to undertake activities which are part of your induction, including observations of colleagues, team-teaching, meeting key members of staff and undertaking continuing professional development (CPD). These activities have the potential to devour a lot of time, meaning that it is important to use free periods effectively so that you don't find yourself sitting up at 10 pm shedding blood, sweat and tears over a lesson for the following day.

Although English teaching has always been associated with high workload, you should still be able to complete most of your duties within the normal working day, with some 'reasonable additional hours'. The Department for Education's 2019 workload survey indicated that the average secondary teacher is completing 13.1 out-of-school hours per week. Although this is still very high (and some might argue, unreasonable), there are some concrete ways to save time and reduce the chances of having to take your work home with you.

Own your space

Simple classroom arrangements, like having spare pens on your desk, or embedding rigid routines, like handing out and returning books in less than 30 seconds, can reduce behaviour issues stemming from 'down time' in lessons, resulting in fewer conversations with pupils over break times and maximising every minute of each lesson too.

Diarise everything

It might sound obvious, but the first thing you should do is to get yourself a diary and copy out all the key dates from your school's calendar. There will come times in the year when staff who haven't checked the shared calendar will double-book you. If you have a well-organised diary, this will save any awkward last-minute cancellations. Be strict with how you plan your time too. Look at your week ahead and schedule in meetings, observations and time for self-directed study. Don't allow anything to encroach on this study time – it's part of your entitlement under the ECF and should remain protected.

Use resource sites

Every now and then, especially if you use social media, a post will crop up condemning teachers who use resource sites. As an ECT, you will have to learn to navigate this nonsense and quite rightly ignore it. Resource sites are an excellent way of saving time. After all, whatever lesson you can think of, it's likely that it already exists. Why reinvent the wheel when you could use the time saved for observations, interventions or CPD? Be wary, though: sometimes the temptation to trawl for the 'perfect' resource can mean you spend longer searching than if you'd made it yourself. Weigh up the time you would need to invest to make the resource against the time you might have to spend searching.

Maintaining balance

When beginning a teaching career, it's all too easy to get lost in the seemingly never-ending planning, reading, marking, researching and admin demands of teaching, but just as important as being there for your students is the importance of you being there for you. Losing yourself and the things that make you 'you' benefits no one; and with teacher retention rates startlingly high, something we all need to be aware of is looking after our own wellbeing.

Make time to love your subject

Let's be honest, the texts we study at Key Stage 3 and GCSE are probably a world away from those you studied at degree level, and there's bound to be some really niche section of literature or language that you simply adore. Making time to indulge yourself in books or theatre that don't feel so immediately relevant to the teaching canon will remind you of why you fell in love with English and will enrich you as a teacher.

Hobbies and interests

Outside of English, there are bound to be other things that make you 'you': a sport, craft, hobby or interest that you value and gives you identity. Even if you need to reduce the hours or time you spend on it, making some time – however little – is a sign of you valuing yourself as an individual rather than simply as a teacher.

Exercise

Exhausting as teaching a full timetable can seem, making time to exercise a few times a week will help you to keep your body and mind fit and well. Often we feel tired when, actually, our bodies have a lot more to give, and exercise can capture that energy productively while also providing mental release.

Connect with others

Stay connected to the people you love: use weekends and the school holidays as family and friends 'catch-up' time and make the effort to visit people, have meals out, and refresh your relationships with those you love. Happy you = happy teaching.

For more information and ideas about maintaining balance and wellbeing, look up #teacher5aday on Twitter.

Developing teaching skills

The learning curve in the early stages of the ECT years is undeniably steep; schools are complex places – each and every one has their own routines and quirks. Marry this with the responsibility of helping pupils to master the nuances of the English language and it will probably feel pretty overwhelming. Yes, there will be tips, tricks and flashy gimmicks, but the most important thing to bear in mind is that teaching comes down to three fundamentals that continuously connect: planning, teaching and feedback. These are the three things that you should always be looking to develop.

Planning

Starting the first ECT year is a bit like passing a driving test – suddenly, just because someone deems that you aren't exactly a *threat* to others, you are placed in charge of a vehicle and expected to manoeuvre and make your way in the real world. On some level, that's really quite frightening. One trap which inexperienced colleagues often fall into is to only ever think one lesson ahead; in a way, this makes sense, but it can inadvertently hamper other aspects of your development. The key is to understand how each lesson connects to the week: ask yourself how the skills and knowledge in the following lesson connect with those throughout the week. More widely, also make sure you continually understand how your lessons fit into the topic that you are teaching. So, fundamentally, make sure you reflect on how a lesson fits into the week's lessons, and how that week fits into the weeks and months ahead; in turn, you should give thought to how your pupils are developing their skills over a longer period of time.

Teaching

One thing people will never get tired of telling you in education is that 'the same stuff comes around again and again'. That's not entirely true; advances in cognitive science and psychology are, fortunately, offering teachers opportunities to sharpen things up all the time. Even if things feel similar, we're doing them with increasing understanding all of the time. In truth, the key to improving what happens in your classroom is to always be open to change, and reflective about what does and doesn't work. Learning is fundamentally messy; but reflection gives you a better chance of distinguishing between gimmicks and what *really* works: one thing education is guilty of is finding something that works and then codifying and duplicating it in other classrooms without explaining the pedagogy that underpins it. For now, the key is to understand the importance of keeping things simple: there are some principles that are extremely good bets when it comes to supporting learning. For the best overview that is currently out there, it would be remiss at this point not to mention Barak Rosenshine's (2012) core principles of teaching – as much as anything, this is the perfect place to start.

Feedback

This is very deliberately entitled 'feedback' rather than 'marking'. This is an absolutely crucial distinction. It might be a small thing, but the concept that underpins it is vital; while marking suggests permanence and one-way communication, feedback is diagnostic in nature, and encourages us to see what we do when we write on learners' work. It might sound naff, but when reading your learners' work, you should be continually reflecting about what influence your teaching has had upon the work. Never, ever 'mark' for the sake of it: *always* ask yourself, 'What do they need to do next?' and 'What am I going to do to support this?' Obviously, part of the feedback is to *you* when reading the work. When you sit down to look at a set of books, there will always be that *one* thing that a significant number of your students need support with: that's where your planning for the next lesson should start.

Behaviour management tips and reading the room

Let's start with a story (which may or may not be true): a young first-year teacher was struggling with a particular class of immature Year 8 students. The head of behaviour (a burly, frightening-looking man, actually) is charged with the task of 'supporting' his colleague. He struts in and proceeds to teach a lesson, and all of the pupils comply with very little fuss – he consistently and clearly applies the behaviour policy exactly as it is laid out in the staff handbook: on his way out, he says, 'That's how you do it!' If this (or anything remotely approaching this) happens to you, then the 'advice' you are receiving isn't worth listening to. Pupils respond differently to different adults, and the only way around this is with consistency and fairness. Do not take things too personally! The unavoidable truth is that if you're a new face, or you're slightly younger looking, some pupils will look to test you. It's natural: we all probably did it ourselves at school too. There are certain things that are really useful to know when it comes to managing behaviour, but before we start, please recognise that, while behaviour policies are meant to be transparent and clear for all, they never work that way in practice. It's the relationship that you have with your pupils that underpins what we might term 'behaviour management'. For you to forge those relationships, you have to be able to trust yourself to do so without leaning too heavily on sanctions. This is hard, and you will undoubtedly make mistakes: it's a balance you will have to consistently strike and reflect on.

Having said that, here's some advice many teachers will wish they were given early on: the basic premise of behaviour management is ensuring that pupils do what you want, when you want it. From a purely transactional point of view, that's it in a nutshell. There are three key things to keep in mind: positivity, objectivity and presence.

Positivity

Disclaimer: there must be a distinction between false praise and positive praise. Throwing around false praise is at best patronising, but more likely downright irritating. Reading the room is about creating as much positivity as you can garner: catching the pupils doing the 'right' thing is much more powerful than pointing out the wrong thing. Let's say you need them to have written the date and title within a certain time frame. Shouting at 25 plus pupils won't work: no one has ownership over that chastising – it just creates distance between you and the pupils. Rather, it's better to recognise the pupils who *have* got it right.

Objectivity

If you need to sanction pupils (however large or small), try and frame it as the *pupil's* choice rather than your subjective decision: phrases such as 'OK, I have to do X now' are helpful. No, teaching isn't a popularity contest, but at the same time, it's really important to make sure that sanctions aren't a personal thing, which can be really tricky. Whether or not your school is a 'restorative practice' school, it doesn't matter: pupils need to understand the reasons why – objectively – you gave them that detention or called home. Consistently and calmly asserting your expectations is crucial to establishing yourself as a 'safe' adult. Let's be honest, in many cases, escalating things by shouting or being impolite (however tempting it might be) isn't just poor modelling; it's also sadly something lots of young people are used to at home, and they will respond in kind! As a result, making sure that pupils have a fresh start with a positive 'hello' models behaviour about acknowledging difficulty but moving on.

Presence

A big part of creating the kind of positive culture you desire is about your presence in the room. You needn't be like the big burly man above, but it's worth remembering that pupils always (at least eventually) respond positively to structure and predictability. Doug Lemov's 'strong voice' technique, from his seminal book *Teach Like a Champion* (2015), is a useful start: make a conscious effort to project your voice from your diaphragm rather than your throat – it does help to assert authority. Another useful tip to make sure you have everyone's attention to give instruction is by counting from five down to one. What underpins it is the respect and acknowledgement that you are happy for the pupils to finish whatever they're doing while you are preparing to bring everyone back to focus on you (hint: you can count as slowly as you like, if you know they need a bit more time – this flexibility is useful when pupils are taking too long to do something simple like writing a title).

Making the most of feedback

There are few times in any teacher's career when they will be offered as much support and feedback as when they are in the initial teacher-training and ECT years. Those opportunities to have someone more experienced sit in the room and offer advice and observations from a different perspective are precious and few. It's imperative then that the feedback from those observations is as impactful as it can be.

Depending on the experience (and the nature of the experience, not just the duration) of your mentor, the type and quality of feedback you receive can vary dramatically. There are some key things to look out for though, and clear ways you can direct feedback to increase its impact.

Ask for concrete examples

Ask your observer for specific things you said or did, and for specific examples of the impact they had. The more concrete the feedback, the more you can understand what happened in the lesson. It's OK if you've missed things – being a novice teacher means you're likely to, as your working memory can only focus on a few things, and many of the processes involved in teaching have yet to become automatic – but the more you can understand about what happened, the more awareness you'll have of your own actions.

Recognise the difference between craft and knowledge

Every time we teach, we're synthesising our subject knowledge and our pedagogical knowledge, and balancing the two in order to translate our subject knowledge into learning experiences for our pupils. The two require each other for successful teaching and learning, and cannot exist in isolation. As such, a weakness in one can undermine the success of your teaching. When you receive feedback, explicitly identify and discuss with your observer or mentor whether your subject knowledge needs boosting, or your pedagogical practice needs refining. Understanding which area to focus on will help you to move forward.

Ask for actions

Sometimes feedback can be very grounded in the lesson that has just taken place, rather than focused on future lessons. While it's important to understand the impact of the events and choices of previous lessons, it's futile to focus on what could have happened; instead, time and energy should be spent focusing on how to improve future lessons. Asking for specific actions that will improve your subject knowledge or practice going forward will help you to understand and implement change. These actions could be:

- reading critical essays and articles, such as those on the British Library website

- annotating a chapter, looking at a particular theme or character

- embedding explicit vocabulary teaching in each lesson

- observing a colleague managing whole-class reading

- annotating an extract before you next teach it

- scripting out your questions before going into a lesson.

Go granular

Ask your mentor to break down your targets into granular action steps (look into instructional coaching or the book *Get Better, Faster* by Paul Bambrick-Santoyo for further information). You may need to draw these out through a series of questions, but the more your observer or mentor can articulate the micro-skills and actions that comprise success in your target, the better.

The complexity of English means there are a range of micro-skills and actions involved in every lesson we teach (vocabulary teaching, reading strategies, worked examples, live modelling, behaviour management, metacognition, offering praise, exploring authorial intent, and annotating, to name but a few!), so ask your mentor or observer to offer a specific high-leverage action that you can explore with them, co-planning if necessary – so you can understand what a really *really* good model looks like and how one might work.

You may wish to ask questions such as:

- What different steps do you take when you're modelling?

- What do you find most successful when using worked examples?

- What would you do first to prepare students for…?

- What would you do next?

- What phrasing do you use when…?

- How do you respond to…?

- Which part of this do you feel is most impactful?

- How often do you…?

Action it

Most important of all is to begin implementing your changes as soon as possible. Identify opportunities to put your feedback and new learning into practice while it's still fresh in your mind. As part of your feedback or mentor meeting, look at your timetable and consider the first opportunity you'll have to try things out. Holding yourself accountable for your progress is vital; the more 'set' your next steps are, the more likely you are to follow them.

Follow up

Having identified and worked together with your mentor on precise actions and learning, make sure you request that they look for them in your next observation. Observations are not things that happen *to* us, but can happen *with* us. In fact, research would suggest that the more we feedforward into our feedback, the more likely we are to action it. Before your next observation, mention elements you've been working on, or areas you're unsure of, so that your mentor is informed and can offer praise or support where you feel it will have the most impact to you and your students.

CPD

It's almost a moot point to suggest that as an English ECT you need to be taking professional development opportunities when they arise. After all, every day for an ECT, and arguably all experienced teachers, is a CPD opportunity. Can we ever really know everything about our subject? Can we ever really say that we know the best strategy to deploy in all situations? Probably not. When so new to the profession, it is advisable to play your part in searching for CPD opportunities, though. Your mentor may not always be aware of what opportunities there are available to you and so, as well as it being part of point eight in the Teachers' Standards that you engage proactively with professional learning, it is your moral imperative to seek and take up opportunities.

The Wellcome Trust report, 'Developing great subject teaching', in 2018 found that subject-specific CPD is more effective than generic pedagogic CPD on pupil outcomes. And a similar report in 2013 by TALIS showed that in higher-performing countries, there was more of a focus on subject-specific CPD. It stands to reason, therefore, that as an ECT in English, you need to be searching for opportunities *in your subject*. This is even more important when we consider that, of all English teachers in state-funded secondary schools in 2016, 18.8 per cent did not have a post-A level qualification in English (Department for Education, 2018). For those in this 18.8 per cent, improving subject knowledge and how to deliver content is going to be critical.

Once you achieve QTS, subject-specific tuition seems to stop, and instead, training tends to focus on establishing yourself as an ECT through classroom routines and behaviour management. The onus shifts onto you to read up on the subject in your own time, and unless someone points you in the right direction, how will you know if what you're reading is going to help improve how you teach English?

The Wellcome Trust report defined three areas of subject-based professional development: subject knowledge; pedagogic content knowledge; and understanding how whole-school CPD can be applied to subject areas. What this means is that, while generic CPD has its place (safeguarding, school routines, and so on), you need to regularly spend time with your department, sharing your collective knowledge, experiences and strategies for teaching English.

There are a number of organisations out there that can help with this, most notably Litdrive, an organisation that provides CPD and resources through its website, and the National Association for Teaching English (NATE), an association which aims to 'empower English teachers to inspire young people'. There are a number of other websites which can help support your professional development needs too: Massolit is an excellent website for video lectures; JSTOR offers a diverse range of journals covering many of the literature texts; FutureLearn often provides free courses for teaching various aspects of English; and the British Council's Teaching English website offers webinars, blogs and resources. It is also highly advisable that you familiarise yourself with your exam board's website – many of these offer guidance on how to teach the GCSE and run regular CPD for teachers about the specifications.

Where to next? Life after the ECT years

Before you begin reading this section, it is vital to remember one thing: career progression is highly personal. Genuinely, it happens at a very different pace for everyone, and often for reasons quite out of our own individual control. Many teachers experience successful first and second years, going about their business without fuss and showing that they are capable not only of being wonderful, reflective practitioners, but also that they are willing and enthusiastic to take on additional responsibilities. This is by no means an expectation on the part of their line manager, but it is lovely to see all the same.

Without doubt, the best way to begin to develop and find leadership opportunities dropping onto your lap is just by being reliable, helpful and consistent. This is, for many, the most appealing and surefire method of assessing whether someone is ready to take on additional responsibility. While not feeling as though you should be doing extra things for the sake of it (let's not forget the core business of actually becoming a better teacher to improve the life chances of the students in your classroom), it's important to remember that experiences such as organising trips and giving pupils extracurricular opportunities are all very useful ways of developing leadership skills.

It's important not to allow yourself to be pigeon-holed into a specific route either. By the end of your ECT period, you will likely have a good feel for the areas of school life that you feel you can thrive within – embrace those feelings and look for opportunities to build on this.

Again, social media – especially Twitter – is a very useful means of sharing, learning and looking outwards beyond your school. There is some absolutely staggering stuff going on in schools across the country, and if not just for the networking and friendships, Twitter is a really useful place to join in the conversation and really find out what makes you tick as an educational professional.

Summary

- Build relationships through respect and the recognition that we all contribute to a school's success.
- Make the most of your mentor through engaging proactively with their expertise.
- Proactively prioritise the things that have impact.
- Don't lose 'you' in the midst of developing your teaching persona.
- Do things at your own pace; enjoy the journey.

2

Subject knowledge

*Laura May Rowlands, Davina Canham
and Holly Wimbush*

Introduction

'What's the point in knowing that? You'll never teach it to 9B!'
Many of us have long – and erroneously – subscribed to the
false notion that anyone could teach anything, so long as they
had a decent hook and an engaging manner. How many of us
remember, with a sense of warmth about the cheeks, certain
lessons from our early career involving beach balls, pink feather
boas and Stetson hats? And how many of us then got lost in
what we might call the 'pedagogy pick "n" mix years', where
we attended lots of weekend conferences and joined in lots
of Twitter chats, lighting upon so-called silver bullets, which
appeared to have worked for someone else, and immediately
introduced them to our own classroom, regardless of differences
in context, experience or continuity? Who remembers 'no pens
day'? It was definitely going to work (but sadly, none of the
students did). Letting students write their own objective? Great
way to waste half the lesson. All of this was simply a distraction
from what matters: the knowledge. The fact is, it's all about the

knowledge. Deep, rich, wide, intimate knowledge of the texts on the paper in front of us. Ultimately, better subject knowledge by us as teachers leads to better outcomes for pupils. Subject knowledge is about ensuring we know the texts and topics we are teaching inside out, in order to strengthen, deepen and ignite the love of our subject for our pupils. If not us, who? If not now, when?

Developing subject knowledge

So, how do we develop subject knowledge? Below is a 'route through' approaching a text or topic.

1. Researching a text prior to teaching

In *Reading Reconsidered*, the authors write: 'part of the value of reading is to be able to read and talk about important books that almost everyone else has read' (Lemov et al., 2016). How, as teachers, are we going to do this in a meaningful way if we do not know this text inside out?

So: you're beginning a new class novel and it's not one you've read before. Or, perhaps you have read it but not taught it. First and foremost, you need to undertake multiple readings of a text before beginning critical reading and research. What questions does each reading generate? In her blog 'Reading all the books', Jo Facer talks about how in pre-annotating your copy of the text, 'That hard "thinking work", which I seem to find increasingly hard to do as the term progresses, is already done' (2013). Many teachers find it useful to create a notebook for each text they are teaching in order to collate notes and to prompt research and teaching ideas. It could even be that you come across a 'nugget' online – not necessarily one you 'need' to communicate explicitly to pupils – and also jot it down here. Having a copy of the same version of the text as the students is helpful for making accurate and detailed annotations. Is this the copy you're going to stick under the visualiser? Maybe, and maybe not, depending on the class you have in front of you and the quality of your handwriting. But it's an integral part of the process with which you plan how to communicate the knowledge you have to the pupils in front of you. However, student versions may not always support a critical reading of the text as well as other editions do; for example, does the text have a critical introduction? Are there annotations to support our reading? Does it include short critical essays to enhance our critical reading? Some editions such as Norton Critical Editions and the Arden Shakespeare or Folger editions have these additional features and support nuanced critical reading of the text, which can be invaluable at any level of teaching. Another useful series of books to support the reading and teaching of Shakespeare is the Arden Language and Writing series, which explores key aspects of the plays alongside ideas for further reading and exploration. The Cambridge Guides series is very useful for both GCSE and A level text research, as is The Very Short Introduction series by Oxford University Press. This series also helps with background and contextual study of GCSE set texts.

A side note on the ease of tracking annotations: if you are teaching through an extract, or have the ability to reproduce the whole text, make use of the line reference feature in Microsoft Word. This not only revolutionises your reading 'in class' as per Lemov's approach, known as 'Control the game', in which line numbers are used to aid focus on the text and for quick reference (2015) – 'Kirsty, pick up from line 11' – but also ensures you can easily recall the specifics of the lines you want to zoom in on in a particular lesson as you come to teach it.

2. Contextualising the text

Often, it can feel that context is a bolt-on; a 'nice-to-know' for a text, but not really that important in the scheme of things. After all, what is the point in a Key Stage 3 group understanding the strength needed to lift a longbow before their study of *Henry V*? Why should we teach the majestic plural to a GCSE group studying *Macbeth*? Because knowing these things makes our pupils cleverer. What's more, they lift the level of understanding, allowing pupils to make more meaningful inferences and better analyses. Understanding that Macbeth reverts from the majestic plural, the 'royal we', to using the pronoun 'I' when he is alone cements his role as usurper; a seemingly simple change in pronoun unlocks so much more meaning for pupils when armed with this knowledge. In addition, who are we to know these things and withhold them from pupils? Consider a group with low prior attainment and reading ages below their chronological age. Are they undeserving of the rich knowledge we freely share with the top set? Of course not.

It's important that as English teachers we build a close working relationship with our humanities colleagues. Why? Because we don't teach in isolation. Far from lumping subjects together, a collaboration between English and humanities bears fruit for all. If at all possible, curricula can be aligned so that subjects are teaching congruent topics: at Key Stage 3 this might mean the history department is teaching the slave trade when their colleagues in the English department are investigating diverse voices which may include the speeches of the civil rights movement, for example. If this isn't possible, however, individual teachers can still make themselves aware of what a class is learning in other subjects. Don't underestimate the power of saying, 'When you learned about X in history, you didn't know this was useful here too. Well…'

A powerful way to ensure cohesive understanding within and between texts is a simple historical timeline, placed at the front of every booklet, included on knowledge organisers or stuck into books. But it should not just be cursorily alluded to: the best way to deepen and strengthen understanding is to see these timelines annotated with key events, kings and queens, and dates of published works. Knowing the sequence of events in the pre-war era: the Great War, the General Strike of 1926, the Wall Street Crash, et al., leads to a much richer analysis of the line 'you can ignore all this silly pessimistic talk' in *An Inspector Calls*. Equally, nuggets of knowledge, such as Eric's seemingly throwaway phrase, 'Steady the Buffs!', after Sheila kisses Gerald, referring to the Royal East Kent Regiment (because of the colour of their waistcoats), can be unpicked to reveal Priestley's disdain of aristocratic sayings synonymous with 'keep a stiff upper lip'. Furthermore, the use of maps in English is a vital tool to be harnessed in helping pupils to develop their contextual understanding. Take the study of Shakespeare, for example. Really getting to grips with the pathos of the 'Once more unto the breach...' speech in *Henry V* can be supplemented with a map showing just how far the soldiers were from home; explaining the distance between Verona and Mantua helps to explain just why Romeo's exile was such a heavy punishment in *Romeo and Juliet*.

'But where's the English?' you may be thinking. In a live CPD session, Christine Counsell posed the question: 'How can the natural overlap and mutual support between subjects be made fruitful?' Our humanities colleagues unknowingly provide so much cultural capital and so much enrichment for success in English at GCSE and beyond that it seems a missed opportunity not to join forces and harness the curriculum to serve all of our subjects.

3. Developing big questions or lines of enquiry

Teachers of history and geography often use 'big questions' or 'enquiry questions' as the spine of a unit of work or for over arching lines of development across their curricula. This approach is useful for us as English teachers too. Rather than chopping up a text into meaningless 'learning objectives', overarching 'big questions', although seemingly simple on the surface, provoke us to consider and research further. Ensuring big questions can actually be answered by the text takes thought and careful planning. As teachers, we need to think of the constituent parts to the answer. What concepts or themes do we need to consider; what contextual knowledge do we need to impart; what procedural knowledge must we include?

An example might be: 'How has the writer created a sense of oppression in the exposition of the text?' This is then broken down into a series of lessons around Freytag's pyramid , which outlines the seven key steps in successful storytelling and story structure; setting; mood; genre; and the list goes on. We need to be explicit about the knowledge around this. If this means that we need to do some reading around the history of, say, the dystopian genre or the 'seven basic plots', this will enrich our teaching. Are we suggesting that 9B converses freely about Jungian influences and meta-plot? No – but as teachers, if we have this knowledge at our fingertips, it can only enthuse, enrich and enlighten our teaching.

We then arrive at how best to prepare pupils for answering that 'big question'. Quite separate from the rich and deep knowledge we have imparted to our pupils, how do we now teach pupils to communicate this in their speech or writing? This is an important, but often overlooked, part of answering a 'big question', and we as teachers need to ensure that our subject knowledge in this respect is not lacking. As graduates, we all instinctively 'know' how to structure an essay; how grammar works; how to embed quotation and utilise punctuation for meaning and effect. The nuts and bolts of this are unpicked in later chapters, but it's worth including here that our subject knowledge in this regard cannot be overlooked.

Case study: Laura May Rowlands, head of English, shares how she approached subject knowledge enhancement within her department

Whilst preparing for the return from my second maternity leave during the first national lockdown in the spring and summer of 2020, I began to think about how I might make better use of the department time available to me to focus specifically on the development of our collective subject knowledge – without adding burden to our already considerable workloads.

As a classics graduate teaching English, I have long felt that there were gaps in my knowledge around some of the things my literature, language, media and linguistics graduate colleagues have at their fingertips. This led me to confront the idea that if I, an experienced teacher and department leader, feel this way, then what price everyone else? I thus decided to ensure that all 'admin' work from me as head of department needed to be communicated via a weekly bulletin, to free up the time we had for subject knowledge enhancement, interleaved with refresher CPD on our core pedagogical approaches. I was influenced by James Ashmore and Caroline Clay in *The Middle Leader's Handbook*, who suggest 'department meetings should be about teaching and learning and nothing else'.

Firstly, I shared my rationale in an online department meeting, which meant that I was able to explain how we would use the golden opportunity of department time to read around, digest, and distil subject knowledge in a way we simply hadn't done before, in order to collectively enhance how we approach a text. I led with an example – although we have taught *Henry V* at Key Stage 3 for several years now, it was fairly recently that I discovered the majestic plural (the 'royal we'). A tiny nugget which could just be an interesting fact – until you see how it's abandoned for rhetorical impact when the king declares to his troops, 'I see you stand like greyhounds in the slips...'. We all agreed: this is the sort of knowledge which lifts any reading of the text.

Next, I spent a considerable amount of time looking again at the GCSE specification within my department and working backwards from what I considered necessary for the very highest grades and beyond. I then distilled this into a subject knowledge audit, grouping sections by topic and asking teachers to complete a simple RAG (red, amber, green) exercise, with space for comments. It was crucial here to make it crystal clear that this was not a checking-up exercise, but one which was going to allow for a cohesive plan for collective development. I explained that this would be a confidential document, kept only by me. Nevertheless, I also sought to share my own gaps – something which I have historically struggled with, but key in overcoming the barrier of feeling vulnerable. The analysis of the team's completed exercises allowed me to ascertain whom I could call on to deliver 'mini lectures' on aspects of texts we planned to study during our department meeting time. For example, one teacher who has lived in Japan for many years drew on his deep knowledge of Japanese culture and history to enrich our collective approach to the GCSE literature poem 'Kamikaze'. My excellent deputy head of department drew on the work she did towards a PhD in linguistics to upskill us in grammar. It was empowering and enlivening for us to 'teach' each other!

From these 'mini lectures', we also, as a department, began to put together a spreadsheet of resource links, pulled from the British Library, JSTOR, and other nuggets we've discovered or books I have bought for our burgeoning department library. This isn't intended to be a panacea, but a starting point for development – self-directed reading which is then fed back to the rest of the department.

Where to look; what to find: seeking out sources for CPD

For those of us without access to a university library (online or in person), there are a number of places to start: for example, the British Library website (www.bl.uk), particularly their 'Discover and learn' section, where you will find their 'Discovering literature' section (www.bl.uk/discovering-literature). Here you can find collections of articles supporting the critical reading of many curriculum texts. The British Library team are also very helpful on Twitter (@BL_Learning) and will direct you to specific collections.

The articles commissioned by the British Library are written by respected academics, as well as being linked to other items in the British Library's collections, for example, J. B. Priestley's programme notes for the first British production of *An Inspector Calls* and Wilfred Owen's manuscripts showing his drafting and revisions. These sources support our deeper reading of the texts, as well as providing ideas for further reading. In addition, extracts from the articles are useful for supporting academic reading in class. The British Library articles can provide useful 'enquiry questions' to help us focus on researching a text or topic further, such as the significance of Victorian beliefs about ghosts when researching *A Christmas Carol* or contextualising the individual poems in an exam board anthology with a poet's wider work.

Another very useful online resource is JSTOR, where thousands of academic essays and articles can be found. Full access to the site is by subscription but individual teachers can create a free account which allows access to a specific number of articles per month. If you teach in a school or academy with a sixth form, it could be worth discussing a school subscription so that sixth formers are also supported with their wider academic reading, particularly if they are studying for the Extended Project Qualification (EPQ).

University libraries

If you live near to a university, you may be able to pay an annual subscription as a local user for borrowing books. In addition, it is a good idea to check what access your alma mater is able to provide you as an alumnus or alumna via their online services.

Beyond libraries: using online organisations for researching set texts

In the last few years, text-specific CPD has increased in availability. Here is a list of some organisations with high-quality, text-specific CPD:

- **Massolit** (www.massolit.io): It is worth discussing a Massolit subscription with other departments as it supports a number of subjects. Individual membership is also available.

- **Gresham lectures** (www.gresham.ac.uk): Register for free lectures on set texts and literary themes; a diverse range of subject matter is available.

- **Oxford University podcasts and videocasts** (https://podcasts.ox.ac.uk/keywords/literature): Another free service on a wide range of set texts, literary themes and beyond.

- **Litdrive UK** (https://litdrive.org.uk): A range of subject-specific CPD videos and slideshows by teachers for teachers. For a small annual subscription, you also have access to a library of teaching resources too.

- **BBC** (www.bbc.co.uk/iplayer): The BBC has a range of television programmes, radio shows and podcasts which support textual subject knowledge, both English specific and across the humanities; *In Our Time* and *You're Dead to Me* are merely two examples. The 'search' facility will help you to sort through the treasure trove which is available.

Widening subject knowledge and beyond using podcasts

Tired of listening to the same music playlist on your journey to school? Here is a great opportunity to connect with research and subject knowledge – a podcast. Many of the following can be accessed via the regular platforms and they often invite other experts to panel a particular subject. Here are some that you should check out: Naylor's Natter; The Leadership Podcast; History Hit Network; The Evidence Based Education Podcast; Mind the Gap: Making Education Work Across the Globe.

Utilising department knowledge

It is not only through our own personal subject knowledge development that we can empower and enable ourselves, our departments and our students, but it can also be through the use of internal subject knowledge via the fantastic colleagues we work with day to day. There is a wealth of experience and knowledge within our faculties that we must make use of, whether this is through sharing expertise and best practice or just utilising department knowledge, as explained in the case study on page 35. A different way to encourage this is through the use of a TeachMeet – a 10-minute get-together where the whole faculty can focus on one element of subject-specific knowledge to develop and explore in more detail by relying on experts within the faculty. It can be factored into faculty meetings or it can be a stand alone meeting one day at school, as it can be brief. A schedule can be sent out for half term and other colleagues can be encouraged to sign up to do their own TeachMeet in order to share their best practice and expertise. This can also lead to knowledge-driven collaborative planning, as well as focusing on implementing elements of pedagogy. Although many subject-knowledge-driven sessions focus on GCSE texts, a faculty can highlight an area of development through a subject-knowledge audit (SKA) that may be completed alongside a curriculum review. This will not only highlight areas of great expertise within your faculty, but it will also highlight areas for development. For example, a faculty may be secure in the knowledge of *Macbeth* but is aware of certain biblical allusions from that text that they may need to research and develop. This would then frame a ten-minute TeachMeet where the faculty can develop this particular element of knowledge in more detail.

After all, as Dylan Wiliam (2019) says, 'Every teacher needs to improve, not because they are not good enough, but because they can be even better.' It is through this principle alone that we can develop teacher quality as it ultimately advances student outcomes.

Subject communities

As teachers, we all share a collective vision and that is to empower and enable all. We should look past our faculty and consider further expertise and knowledge from our local area – primary schools, other secondary schools, sixth-form colleges and universities. By reaching out and constructing a network of support and knowledge, we can not only share our expertise, but also develop a collegiate community. If you do not already have this as part of your wider school focus, or your school is not part of an academy chain, you can nurture a network by emailing local schools in your vicinity and inviting them to join you to discuss a particular area of development or strength that they could lead on via a TeachMeet or a hub meeting. A further untapped resource is utilising university subject knowledge. With university numbers decreasing, institutions are very willing to support and ease the transition from A level to academia. This is also a wonderful opportunity to stretch and challenge higher-graded students at GCSE. Universities offer a range of open days, lectures to students and even open discussions on elements of A level and GCSE courses. This has become easier to manage due to remote learning and video conferencing in light of Covid-19. There is now a wealth of resources for teachers to utilise that come from not only local but also national, if not international, subject communities. Online subject communities are just as powerful. For example, on Twitter you can find a rich and diverse network of collegiate voices such as @Team_English1 (who also arrange a fantastic annual national conference); @EngChatUK (a weekly discussion on all things English, run by @agwilliams9); @LitDrive (a charity driven by providing subject knowledge, professional development and resources); @ResearchEd; @DiverseEd; @MTPTProject; @TMEnglishIcons; @TeacherDevTrust; @CLiC_fiction. By connecting to a broader range of voices via social media, you can be at the forefront of new research, resources and pedagogy.

Developing subject knowledge for A level

Studying English literature at A level is in many ways to study the human condition. A level should be valued as a seven-year journey of conversations writers want to have about the world; not something that only happens from Year 11. A level teachers are role models for their department and share their knowledge of texts, contexts and writers with their department. A level tests greater breadth, depth and nuanced understanding, so subject knowledge is key.

A level uptake

Since English is a core subject, it can get overlooked in a student's A level choices. English teachers have in recent years noticed a decline in the uptake of A level English. So what can we do to raise the profile of our subject to be something pupils see as a viable choice for A level?

Start early, ideally from Year 7. Drop comments into your Year 7 lessons such as, 'This is the same poet we study at A level' or, 'The elements of Gothic we are looking at are something you can look forward to building on at A level.' Year 10 is a good place to really embed this. Inviting interested candidates to a screening from The National Theatre or Royal Shakespeare Company (RSC) with a research task or project linked in can be effective. Furthermore, you could invite some current A level students to visit English lessons and give a presentation or question-and-answer session on A level English. Using sixth formers as advocates for A level English certainly can add weight; therefore, ask some to come and speak to potential students at your sixth-form open evening. Finally, many universities now hold online taster courses or competitions for younger pupils, which often really challenge them to be creative or engage in real-world topics.

Transition from GCSE to A level

Starting to study English literature at A level can feel like a different world altogether. Students can feel it is a huge jump in expectations and independent workload. One consideration is to have the most accessible content at the beginning of the A level curriculum. Starting with unseen prose or poetry can help to bridge the gap between what students did for GCSE and what we expect at A level. It is also a good way for students to recap key disciplinary knowledge. What has become increasingly popular is to set a transition project for pupils over the summer holidays to lessen the step change. Researching the contexts of a core text can be a good way to get students immersed. This research can be guided by the teacher to certain areas and through questions with links to websites. Take *The Help* by Kathryn Stockett, for example, which is historical fiction set in 1960s Jackson, Mississippi, but published in 2009. Students could research the American civil rights movement, Medgar Evers, and Jim Crow laws. For literary context, students could research many of the intertextual allusions in the novel, such as *To Kill a Mockingbird* by Harper Lee or *Invisible Man* by Ralph Ellison. Indeed, students could also research multiperspectivity since the novel is told by three narrators.

Poetry of a particular genre or literary movement can be an appropriate transition introduction for students. Link to the theme, genre or socio-historical context studied at A level, but focus on different poets to those covered by the set text. Independent wider reading is key for A level. Giving pupils links to critical reading on the web and introducing them to key websites teachers might want them to use over the course of their A level studies is vital to their success.

You could also provide students with a reading list that includes the set texts they will study throughout the course as well as making intertextual links to the canon surrounding the studied texts. It will encourage a wider reading and understanding of typicality and atypicality whilst also developing their understanding of the authors' contemporaries and how particular themes are inherent throughout literary study.

The non-exam assessment (NEA)

Sell pupils the real positives they can benefit from completing this piece: working independently and researching books they really love. This can be something immensely personal to students as it offers them the chance to discuss and enthuse about texts – it provides a sense of independence from the constraints of predilection. This is truly an opportunity for students to flourish and exercise their own literary critic. Furthermore, highlight how refining their essay skills will improve essay-writing in other subjects. Another plus side is that it's great practice for university assignments. The NEA is worth a percentage of the final A Level. This means that pupils can have about 20 per cent of their A level grade under their own control. This can be a very motivating factor.

The texts

Often the NEA piece needs to be a comparison of two texts from two different authors. Different exam boards have their own rubrics and it is best to check the specification you follow. For some, for example, one text has to be pre-1900 (both can be) and can be from any genre: prose, play or poetry collection. Often, exam boards have a list of suggested texts and sometimes, a list of texts you cannot use since they are exam texts. When choosing texts, school context and individual students are key. Ideally, you will have students who are voracious, independent readers who know what they want to study and might have even read one or two of their chosen texts already. More often than not, however, students need more help than this.

One idea could be to choose one core class text to focus on. This depends on your students, but choosing a core text from pre-1900 can be helpful as students might be less likely to read pre-1900 texts, or some simply find them intimidating.

To have a core text and some nudges to key moments and themes is really helpful. As a springboard, this can give students confidence to approach another text as they have some models and strategies for how to start on the second book. Additionally, it can be helpful to get students to search the internet for themes or ideas in their first book and see which other books contain similar ones. Develop a pre-made list of potential books with concepts linked to each one. That way students may start to see links more easily between texts in terms of theme, character, genre or narrative structure.

Once texts have been chosen, students need to assemble a body of key moments, arguments, quotations and other notes about their texts. It can be useful to draw up a schedule of what notes should be produced when. Tasks for a schedule might include:

- character studies
- chapter summaries
- theme studies
- key moments with reasoning and evidence
- timelines
- narrative structure and perspective
- relevant context research and genre features
- critical reading.

A good starting point can be for students to compare the opening couple of pages of each text and consider:

- What are we being told about events and character, and why?

- What is the author withholding?

- Why this setting?

- Why this narrative perspective?

- What interests you about the opening most of all?

At A level, students are expected to come up with their own texts, topics and essay questions. Good starting points are: themes, characterisation, genre, and finally, what is the big conversation writers want to have with their respective audiences? Some areas students might focus on are:

- the Gothic

- satire and dystopia

- war and conflict

- representations of race and ethnicity

- representations of sexuality

- representations of gender

- representations of power

- representations of identity

- representations of social class and culture.

Creating questions

For the NEA, students have to design their own question based on their own interests and with teacher guidance. For example, having a viewpoint before the question can help:

*' "Women in literature are often portrayed as weak victims."
In light of this view, compare and contrast the ways
[insert text titles] present women and to what extent they
are victims.'*

This style of question sets up the possibility of a debate. Key
also is the phrase 'the ways', as it focuses clearly on analysis
of methods that a writer uses to convey their ideas. Run
draft questions by the exam board advisor assigned to your
school. Teachers can receive objective opinion and feedback
on the suitability of student questions, and next steps can
be to have mini tutorials in a follow-up lesson to discuss any
question tweaks.

Planning NEA essays

Students need to be encouraged to spend time in lessons
planning their main arguments. They could draw up a list of
main links, or similarities and differences between the texts
focused on their question steer. Now students can look to see
if these could be grouped together or ordered into a logical
argument. They then use these sections to plan each argument
and might note down: key moments, quotations, relevant
methods or context, analysis, effects and any of their critical
reading. Only once they have planned out sections can they
start writing.

Critical reading and literature reviews

Students need directing towards some critical reading to
inform their ideas. Articles from the English and Media Centre,
JSTOR, the British Library, *Guardian* interviews and reviews
can all help, and Massolit have a superb suite of literature

lectures. Universities are also very happy to support, with many suggestions of critical reading posted on their websites or you can always email for advice. One strategy could be to direct students to links you have found and ask them to summarise the main arguments and three golden nugget quotations as takeaways to be cited later. Further research on their chosen topic is key; it could be that as a homework task you set students a literature review. Students go away and research what has been written already on the aspect or theme they are interested in, and summarise salient points and their own thoughts about their possible arguments or areas of focus. At this point it is probably a good idea for them to start a bibliography to track their reading and sources.

Critical perspectives

Gauging a critical response to literary texts is as important as the original texts themselves. It is essential that students pay reference to what has gone before and can therefore engage with criticism. Through their discussion of themes, students can become aware of certain schools of theory. For example, when reading Margaret Atwood's *The Handmaid's Tale*, students become aware of a feminist theoretical reading due to the depiction of suppressed women in the text. It is through the teacher that students can ultimately connect with theoretical principles of literary criticism. Introduce students to the following literary theories alongside your chosen texts: Marxism; psychoanalysis; feminism; postcolonialism; structuralism; poststructuralism; postmodernism. If you teach combined language and literature at A level, you will want to signpost students to stylistics and its overlapping subdisciplines, such as literary stylistics, evaluative stylistics, discourse stylistics, feminist stylistics and cognitive stylistics. One of the main advantages of applying theory to a literary text is the development of interpretation which allows students to connect to critical discussions, helping students to become perceptive and assured in their essay-writing.

It is worth noting that students do not have to mention lots of critics' quotes. Indeed, students can refer to a performed version's interpretation of their text or their own alternative perspective. Furthermore, this can be an aspect of an essay where students struggle. Often, students do tend to choose a quotation they either do not understand or do not unpick; or worse, a quotation that does not relate to their argument at all. It must be made clear that the quotation needs to illuminate their argument; not simply be thrown in and left there. A way to combat this is for students to spider diagram the reference they want to use. First they summarise what the quotation is stating. Next they state how it links to their argument, and then list what evidence or examples they have to support or refute it. Exam boards have also made note of how often students make sweeping statements about feminism or patriarchal society, for example. A way round this could be to ensure you have taught some mini lessons on relevant theoretical perspectives (feminist, Marxist or new historicist) so that students can plan them relevantly into their arguments.

Summary

- Subject knowledge development should be an ongoing process throughout your teaching career.
- Utilise external sources; there are so many available.
- Utilise your department's collective knowledge.
- Consider your approach to A level subject knowledge development carefully.

3

Planning and assessment

*Kaley Macis-Riley, Laura May Rowlands,
Lyndsay Bawden and Mary Hind-Portley*

Introduction

What do you want your pupils to learn, and how do you know
if they have learnt it? These are two of the most fundamental
questions you can ask yourself as a teacher; as an English
teacher the answers are not always straightforward. The
domain of English knowledge is huge, and we do not have
enough time in our finite lesson hours to cover everything, so
carefully selecting what we consider to be the most powerful
knowledge, which will bring the most benefits, is essential.
But there are wide differences in what is deemed essential
and powerful, and it's unlikely that you and your colleague in
the next classroom will agree on every element. And when
we've finally decided what that knowledge is, how is it to
be assessed? How do we judge pupils' work formatively,
as part of a feedback and action cycle, so we can identify
gaps and misconceptions, and re-teach? How do we assess
summatively in a way which is objective, sampling the whole

domain, and which is normed and standardised so the results are accurate and meaningful?

We delve into these questions more deeply in this chapter.

Research and theory

The meaning of assessment

For too long, assessment was onerous, unproductive and useless. We did it, but we didn't use it. It was – without sounding too unprofessional – arbitrary. Teachers would spend hours inputting assessment data, but how did we truly use it? We need to take back the control of assessment and be confident in our use of it as a way to support pupils. What gaps do they have? What do I need to re-teach? Where are the misconceptions? How can I support that pupil in developing that particular part of their work? How can I show them this?

This doesn't mean giving them a question and 45 minutes to respond to it, followed by a number out of x and a grade which serves no purpose but to distract pupils from the very point of your spending time with their work: feedback, feedback, feedback.

Let it be said that for us to successfully assess our pupils' development of powerful, cultural knowledge, Key Stage 3 is not in place to over-practise GCSE-style tasks and be marked with GCSE-style criteria. If we do this, we restrict our pupils.

English is not simply our GCSE content. It is so much more than that, and Key Stage 3 has to offer the breadth of knowledge needed to understand the confines of GCSE, but also the world beyond. We must provide pupils with the breadth and depth that provides them with the freedom that they need to succeed – and that doesn't mean a question every week from a

GCSE paper 'adapted' to suit their age category, which we use to assess their understanding of our subject.

Granted, when the new specification exams came out in 2015, the boards confused us with their 'Key Stage 3 exams', which were – actually – just GCSE papers on 'more accessible' texts such as *The Boy in the Striped Pyjamas*, but the overall consensus from those schools that used these 'Key Stage 3 exams' was that they were a complete waste of time and they told us absolutely nothing to support our pupils or our teaching moving forward. Surely reflective teaching is the very purpose of assessment, is it not?

Not only do we end up losing our pupils, and their interest and love for a subject that we too love, but we learn nothing about them. GCSE-style assessments are not made for Key Stage 3 pupils. Therefore, by assessing them with such tools, we learn – at best – very little and – at worst – nothing. We hone our focus on what GCSE equivalent they should be getting, rather than what we want them to know, why and when.

If your school policy is to use GCSE-style assessments, then don't be afraid to address this as a concern to your curriculum leaders. It is the middle leaders who are the go-between for SLT and teaching staff. Most schools are moving away from this idea of 'GCSE lite' at Key Stage 3, but many are not. Provide a solution to a problem that you see, and address it with professionalism, whilst also providing solid examples; you'll be surprised at the impact you can have.

Moving forward from data-driven assessments

This attitude towards assessment is – thankfully – beginning to change. Thanks to the new Ofsted (2019) framework moving towards curriculum and pedagogy, rather than data-based targets and spreadsheets that hide away for years until the inspectors descend, we are beginning to see assessment in a new light: one which shines on our teaching and learning, tells us about our pupils in a way that supports their trajectory of progress, and one which develops us as educators and school leaders.

As Dylan Wiliam (2014) says, 'validation is *the* central concept in assessment' and it is 'really important… that we are hardly ever interested in how well a student did on a particular assessment. What we are interested in is what we can say, from that evidence, about what the student can do in other situations, at other times, in other contexts.' If we are making inferences about a pupil in Key Stage 3, based on the expectations of pupils at the end of Key Stage 4, then we will be getting it wrong. We have to ensure that the inferences that we – as teachers – make of an assessment are validated.

We must first separate the formative and the summative. Formative is our tool to find out, constantly, what it is that pupils know and don't know. Summative is a judgement about whether or not a pupil is on track. That doesn't need to be on some ridiculous flightpath – because progress isn't linear. And it doesn't need to be converted into an 'equivalent GCSE grade' for their age, because they are not GCSE pupils.

Our assessments must be meaningful, and must inform our future planning. Where are our pupils right now? What have they missed, and where do they need to be?

The purpose of assessment is not to enter numbers into a spreadsheet, but to help us to help our pupils. Therefore, we must use it to assess the retention of knowledge and the application of that knowledge, and it should not be based on a future exam they are likely to sit.

If assessments are merely seen as a tool for data, then 'teaching to the test is more likely to happen' and that's when we 'don't focus on teaching knowledge' (Christodoulou, 2017a).

Putting it into practice

Planning a curriculum

How does one actually go about designing a curriculum? First you need to establish a vision to underpin and drive the decisions you make about the content, so that you're in a position to ask yourself the right questions about content and sequencing, and be able to answer those questions in an informed way.

The next question you need to ask yourself is: what powerful knowledge do I need to teach? Knowledge is generative, and the function of this powerful knowledge is to enable pupils to, as Bernstein says, 'think the unthinkable'. So what is that powerful knowledge in English? Is it Shakespeare? Is it Romantic poetry? Is it sentence structure? Is it rhetoric? You have a finite amount of time in the curriculum so you have to select what goes in carefully, and what is left out, and be able to articulate your rationale behind those choices.

We can break that idea of powerful knowledge down even further: to start with, there's core knowledge. This is the knowledge you want pupils to remember in the long term; it's the foundational knowledge we hang other knowledge on. It might be, for example, that sentences begin with a capital letter and end with a full stop. It might be that stories have a beginning, a middle and an end. Whatever you decide the core knowledge is in English, it must be returned to and built upon in a systematic, repetitive way, to enable pupils to build a strong schema (mental models) to underpin their future learning.

Hinterland learning refers to the extras, the stories – putting flesh on the bones of the core knowledge. For example, the core might be the plot, the characters, the structure of a novel – the bits we can reduce down to the A4 page of the knowledge organiser; the hinterland is reading and enjoying the whole novel, lingering over the words, journeying with the characters. And you need to decide what hinterland knowledge you will teach and why, and what you have to leave out and why, and be clear what hinterland is *not*. Christine Counsell (2018) tells us: 'It helps us distinguish between a vital property that makes the curriculum work as narrative and merely "engaging activities" which can distract and make pupils think about (and therefore remember) all the wrong things. It allows teachers to have this kind of conversation: "Isn't that a distraction?" "No, it's hinterland. This is why..."' You want hinterland knowledge to pique the curiosity and intellect of pupils, to foster a passion for English – not because of gimmicky 'fun' lessons, but because of the power and beauty of the knowledge you are imparting.

Substantive knowledge is another area to consider. Substantive knowledge is the hard facts of the domain. In English, we have less uncontested substantive knowledge than science or maths, for example; this makes deciding what we teach sometimes contentious. When you are choosing which substantive knowledge to teach, you need to ask yourself how it will develop pupils' existing schema, how it will link into the key themes of the curriculum, how rich and beautiful it is, and if it fits with your curriculum vision.

Threshold concepts are the key ideas that allow pupils to access the next stage of their learning, and without which they cannot progress. An example is that pupils must master the idea of characters as constructs – so many pupils are held back by writing as if characters and plots are real, and until they grasp the contrived and crafted nature of a character as a construct, they cannot move on to meaningful understanding of writers' choices and analysis of effect. To plan an effective curriculum, you need to identify what these threshold concepts are, when to include them, how to explain them, and when and how to return to them to reinforce and develop them, because of course these are likely to be complex and difficult ideas which will require repeated exposure to in order to be fully understood and for pupils to be able to apply them.

Disciplinary knowledge means how we address English as a study, a discipline and a tradition, outside of the subject in school; how it moves beyond the curriculum, and has a value of its own outside of those institutions. Think about which aspects of English you studied at university – how do they influence what you deliver in the classroom? How well prepared for that disciplinary study were you by your English lessons in school? A consideration for us should be: how do we address this in our teaching? For example, this means teaching our pupils how and why it's important to respond in an academic style, and to be critical consumers of text, thus bringing what happens in our classrooms closer to the study of the discipline itself. Another example of disciplinary knowledge we need to consider is the influence of societal movements on literature, for example, the French Revolution on the Romantics. So it's about giving pupils the sense that the subject doesn't exist, as Claire Hill and Kat Howard put it, in a vacuum, that 'social, cultural and political shift are mirrored by the work of that time' (2020), and that literature is interpreted as reflecting norms and values, and as revealing the ethos of culture, the processes of class struggle, and certain types of social 'facts'. This then opens the door to looking at power structures, decisions and influences – who decides what is valuable and important?

Procedural knowledge is knowing how to complete a task or to demonstrate knowledge. We need to be deliberately consistent in our teaching of procedural knowledge in order to reduce the impact of learning new methods on pupils' working memory. For example, have you taken over a class and tried to do a what/how/why analysis of a section of text, only to be faced with a chorus of 'that's not how we normally do it!'? This detracts from the substance of the task and impedes pupils' mastery of the process. It's the same with terminology: do you use 'discourse markers' or 'connectives'? Through consistency, we give a sense of cohesion and commonality to the curriculum, as well as ensuring equity of experience. Consider: what procedural knowledge do you need to prioritise, and how do you teach it in a consistent way?

We must ensure that the powerful knowledge we teach is sequenced in a cohesive way, that one unit connects to another, so even though the content is different, we are revisiting and building on the concepts of the discipline. For example, you might wish to follow a mostly chronological sequence, as that makes it easier for pupils to see the evolution of the subject and the influences one period of time and its writers have on the next generation. In relation to cognitive load, this helps to reduce the load on working memory because a chronological sequence allows us to draw on and activate prior knowledge in a systematic and logical way in order to apply it to the new learning. When we make explicit the connections between the prior knowledge and the new knowledge, it strengthens pupils' schema. This is why, for example, many teachers teach the poems 'Ozymandias' (Percy Bysshe Shelley) and 'London' (William Blake) before they teach *Jekyll and Hyde* or *A Christmas Carol*; it allows pupils to use that prior knowledge to deepen their understanding of the next knowledge in the curriculum.

Planning for conceptual development within and across an English curriculum

What concepts and constructs should underpin an English literature curriculum? Firstly, what is a concept? What is a construct? We will consider these in abstract terms before considering concrete examples.

Concept: an idea or mental image which corresponds to some distinct entity or class of entities.

Construct: an idea or theory containing various
   conceptual elements.

Mary Myatt refers to concepts as 'holding baskets', helping us to group facts, make sense of multiple pieces of information and see the connections between them. They become an efficient way for us to make sense of these 'multiple pieces of information'. For experts, they become intellectual shorthand and we need to help pupils to use this shorthand efficiently and effectively.

Concepts are largely, but not exclusively, expressions of important ideas within an academic discipline. Our pupils are entitled to know them and to use them. Concepts enable connections to be made across a disparate range of facts; they reside in the long-term memory and can be called on to make sense of new information. Concepts provide the intellectual architecture on which new knowledge and insights can be pinned.

For example, as teachers we may talk confidently about the narrator or narrative voice in a text, which we class as a concept. However, when we discuss 'narrative voice' in more general terms, we begin to move to a construct, as we need to employ other concepts to understand what narrative voice is, such as first- and third-person narrative viewpoint.

The National Curriculum document does not explicitly refer to the specific terms 'concepts' and 'constructs', but it does outline what the curriculum should cover; knowing the National Curriculum for English in detail is essential and any planning activity should have this to hand. In addition, we should also consider those concepts we consider to be threshold concepts as originated by Land et al. (2006). We need to decide what are our 'jewels in the curriculum'. 'A focus on these jewels,' write Land et al., 'allows for richer and more complex insights into aspects of the subjects students are studying; it plays a diagnostic role in alerting tutors to areas of the curriculum where students are likely to encounter troublesome knowledge and experience conceptual difficulty.'

Once we understand the idea of concepts, threshold concepts and constructs, we can focus on building strong schema for our pupils through our English curriculum.

In the following sections, we outline a range of concepts for you to consider, either at the whole-curriculum level, within units or within your own lessons.

Reading narrative

What concepts relating to reading narrative could be explored over time? Here are some examples:

- narrative voice and perspective
- reliability and unreliability
- plot: the seven basic plots
- story structure
- Propp, Vonnegut, and others of the structuralist and Russian Formalism schools
- motif and trope
- literary allusion and intertextuality
- inference, implication and ambiguity.

Narrative voice and perspective

In order for pupils to understand how stories are told, what do we teach them about narrative voice and perspective? What do they know about first, second and third person, and omniscient narrator? How do we teach pupils to distinguish between the author and the narrator? What understanding of grammar, syntax and sentence structures support pupils in understanding the construction of a narrative voice? These are the questions we pose as part of revising and constructing a curriculum. How strong is our understanding as teachers of narrative voice and do we have a common understanding of how this is taught across a department? Which aspects of literary theory do we need to discuss and explore as teachers as part of our ongoing subject-specific CPD? How do the texts we want to teach help our pupils to understand narrative voice? How do we look at increasingly complex narrative perspectives?

Plot

The work of Christopher Booker (2004) has been very influential on many teachers' approach to teaching plot and structure, alongside John Yorke's *Into the Woods* (2014). Exploring the seven basic plots explicitly with pupils, as part of a storytelling unit, will support their own creative writing, because then they are working with a literary framework of universal stories, in the European tradition at least. If we pair this with exploring the Freytag (1894) model of dramatic structure, we can build a strong schema around the concept of plot. Once pupils have a general understanding of the seven basic plots, we can then move on to discussing structure of the narrative and narrative voice. When exploring isolated elements in order to develop a specific theoretical understanding, we must always root such theory in concrete examples of story, for example, linked to Greek myths, fairy tales and the chosen novel, so that we create strong connected knowledge across the curriculum. In addition, Vonnegut's story structures, from his rejected Master's thesis in anthropology, can support pupil understanding further. His lecture can be accessed at openculture.com/2011/04/the_shape_of_a_story_writing_tips_from_kurt_vonnegut.html. There is obviously much more to explore about the concept of plot and the different literary theories, which cannot be dealt with here.

Motif and trope

Once we have considered narrative voice, plot and structure as part of curriculum planning, we could then consider how and where we develop our pupils' understanding of motif and trope. These act as shorthand within texts and carry considerable interpretive weight within a narrative. If pupils cannot read motifs and tropes, their inference and analytical understanding are hampered; we need to consider how we teach these both explicitly and in context, and consider how confident we are as teachers in identifying motifs and tropes, particularly reading outside the Western canon. As part of the curriculum-planning process, common motifs can be identified and discussed, supported by critical reading. By planning deliberate encounters through the entire curriculum, we are preparing our pupils to become confident critical and analytical writers, which they can then demonstrate in an exam context.

Literary allusion and intertextuality

To support our pupils' understanding of literary allusion and intertextuality, we need to consider the sequencing of texts within our English curriculum. However, this is not about reducing the curriculum to a reductive list of allusions, more that we consider how our text choices develop our pupils' specific and wider understanding of literary allusions and their use as narrative devices. Therefore, in our long-term planning, we need to consider our core literature texts. How do they support our pupils' experience with story and narrative to develop their understanding of the common allusions? As teachers, are we confident of our own understanding of allusions and their origins, for example, Pandora's box and Dante's circles of hell? As experienced and sophisticated adult readers, we connect earlier texts with newer texts and see the influences of past literature on succeeding writers. We need to consider how we create connections for pupils between texts through our text choices and where we locate them in the curriculum.

Inference, implication and ambiguity

This section has been placed at the end of this section because inference is dependent on our knowledge of texts and how writers work. As teachers, we need to be very clear about the conceptual difference between inference (the action of the reader) and implication (the action of the writer) and how these work in the acts of reading and writing. Therefore, it is important that, as curriculum planners, we ask ourselves a number of questions as part of the curriculum-planning process:

- How do our text choices and the sequence of our texts build an increasingly sophisticated interpretation of text through the act of inference, at key points in a text and across the narrative of a text?

- How do our text choices support an increasingly sophisticated understanding of implication and the ways writers construct implication?

Once we know the answers to these questions, we are in a better position to support our pupils' understanding of deliberate ambiguity and why writers employ this technique as part of their relationship with their reader.

*

The list of concepts outlined above is not comprehensive; it does not include constructs such as the hero or the tragic hero, for example, which are also part of our consideration when curriculum planning. Also, you will see that we have not outlined a solely linear sense of progression. In terms of progression, conceptual understanding should not be atomised into a series of assessment statements, but rather written into the choices of texts over the time of the pupils' curricular experience so that we support pupils on their journey as confident, competent and critical readers.

While we have outlined some key literary concepts here, we would also encourage you to explore the philosophical concepts present in your curriculum linked to your text choices, such as power, duty, honour and responsibility. You could:

- review your current curriculum, and identify the philosophical concepts which appear most frequently

- consider which additional philosophical concepts could be explored to deepen reading and benefit pupils when they encounter 'unseen' texts.

Long-term planning

This sequencing of the knowledge of the curriculum should form the basis of your long-term curriculum planning. Once you have listed and sequenced your knowledge and key concepts, and devised a mission statement for your curriculum, long-term planning puts flesh on the bones, and is the fun part where in English we decide which materials and hinterland we will use to impart the key knowledge we have decided to teach.

This document is one you should be able to share with other teachers for them to use as a framework for their medium-term and lesson-planning. Therefore, it must contain key guidance about the core elements of the curriculum, as a starting point:

- sequencing of core, threshold and procedural knowledge

- number of weeks assigned to each unit

- the big questions or core concepts being explored in each unit

- Tier 2 and 3 vocabulary to be explicitly taught

- contextual knowledge to focus on.

A simple table is often the best way to structure this, as it is easy to read and not as intimidating as a page of text might be.

Medium-term planning

When considering how to connect the black dots and create that map from the learning at primary level to the learning at secondary level, we must meticulously plan our schemes of work with precision.

As Christine Counsell (2018) says so wisely, 'But the curriculum itself is the progression model. Its mastery is progress. That is what it is for. When it comes to progress, the burden of proof is on the curriculum.' So, if we don't plan our schemes of work with precision and deep thinking, how do we know if pupils are making progress?

In order to plan effectively, we must first ask ourselves: what do we want our pupils to know? When? Why? We do this, as mentioned in the section above, when planning our curriculum. It's the finer detail that comes into play when we consider our medium-term plans. There has to be a clear map of knowledge, where – as those responsible for putting these plans in place – we can see the links and we can justify the precise time that they take place: what do our students need to know, remember, and use in the future?

Once upon a time we lived in a world where planning schemes of work was based on what was in the cupboards, what we enjoyed teaching and what we think would 'hook' the pupils in – graphic novel unit, anyone? Grammar through film?

Such approaches have, thankfully, started to become less common, but curricula in which links across the key stages are difficult to see, in which 'GCSE lite' units are dominant at Key Stage 3, and in which cumulative knowledge is not given a thought, still exist. In order to create competent, culturally literate adults of the future, we must work hard to develop an approach to curriculum that exposes them to an array of powerful knowledge, not just what we want them to learn, or that trains children to be exam monkeys. To quote David Holbrook: 'We have no need to concern ourselves with education for "earning a living": we educate for living.' We must consider, when planning schemes of work and our way through them via medium-term planning, that we are creating young people with an array of knowledge and skill to apply said knowledge, who can hold articulate and intellectual conversations with their peers. It is our moral obligation to provide pupils with the means by which they can live and thrive successfully in the complex world in which they find themselves.

Next steps for curriculum planning

- Consider your priorities for your curriculum content and write a vision statement to encapsulate them.
- List the nine to 12 core topics you would teach over Key Stage 3; what's the best sequence for them and why?
- What core, substantive, disciplinary and procedural knowledge do you need to include, and why? Where should they go?

Medium-term planning: how to get it right

When taking a curriculum overview, we must really start to analyse our choice of unit, text and key concept. We must *overthink* the schema and make constant links back to our curriculum intent. Our medium-term plan is our implementation of that intent, and the two must be inextricably linked.

The blueprint to every English curriculum must be that we teach pupils about the world that was, the world that is, and the world that will be. But not only this: we must also teach children about their place in that world and how it belongs to them just as much as it belongs to anybody else.

While a long-term plan, often known as a 'curriculum overview' (see Figures 3.1, 3.2 and 3.3 on the following pages), allows us to map out the general journey, it is the medium-term planning that truly allows us to consider the all-important *how*. What about the world do your cohorts need exposing to? What about history is it important for your community of pupils to understand in order to understand themselves and their own importance? The demographic within which you teach will be different to the one in which colleagues in another part of the country teach, and that's where local needs and the importance of well-rounded, powerful schemata of knowledge work hand in hand.

Figures 3.1, 3.2 and 3.3 show an example of a medium-term plan for a Key Stage 3 English curriculum that takes these points into consideration.

As a classroom teacher, you may feel like you have little control over the curriculum and deciding what students need to know and when, but it is important that curriculum design is a team effort. It is worth reading up on, looking into and initiating a discussion with your curriculum leader(s). Many of the best curriculum leaders began as 'just' English teachers, but spoke up about their vision and formulated

		Autumn	Spring	Summer
			Reading for Pleasure strand x 1 per fortnight, explicitly taught grammar lesson x 1 per fortnight. (Final lessons of the week.)	Reading for Pleasure strand x 1 per fortnight, explicitly taught grammar lesson x 1 per fortnight. (Final lessons of the week.)
Year 7		**Where we came from – the origins of our stories**	**Middle English and the Development of Language**	**Introducing Shakespeare at a Secondary School Level**
	Two week transition unit and baseline.			
	Intent	An exploration of stories which provide the basis of our narratives via archetypes, types of narrative and the hero's journey (Odysseus, Achilles, Sampson), to form a basis of understanding of characters but also the idea of allusions to classical and biblical texts. Non-fiction texts will be woven within in order to understand concepts.	An exploration of the formation of human identity and voice. *Beowulf*, the Bible and Chaucer. Linked, unseen non-fiction woven in to further develop knowledge of concepts.	An exploration of sonnets through the ages, and the presentation of romantic/courtly love, familial relationships and honour/pride in *A Midsummer Night's Dream*. Linked, unseen non-fiction woven in to further develop knowledge of concepts. Students will be able to draw on comparisons with the presentation of heroes by WS and those in previously studied texts. Sonnets will be embedded to explore the idea of love in Elizabethan era.
	1Key Concepts	Narrative structures Archetypes (heroes and villains) Allusion Theatre/Audience	Archetypes Allusion Audience Courtly Love	Archetypes Audience Allusion Gender (power) Courtly love/romance Notion of the hero
	Mastering Writing	Vocabulary instruction: aetiological, allusion, anthropomorphism, archetypal, epic, heroism, hubris, metamorphosis, moral, mortal, myth, nemesis, psychological, stereotypical, vengeance Grammar: composing a topic sentence, subject/verb agreement, past and simple tenses.	Vocabulary instruction: Grammar: Using evidence, pronoun ambiguity, prepositional phraseology, run-on sentence, speech punctuation and narrative structures, sentence composition,	Vocabulary instruction: Grammar: temporal clauses, paragraphing, avoidance of fragmented syntax
	Summative assessment	Analysis of extract – inference, evidence. Pre- and post-unit knowledge check (MCQ).	Non-fiction writing: using the written voice to express opinion. Pre-unit knowledge check and cumulative knowledge check (MCQ).	Analysis of extract – inference, evidence, meaning. Narrative writing exploring the journey of a hero. Pre-unit knowledge check and cumulative knowledge check (MCQ).

FIGURE 3.1 *An example Year 7 English curriculum*

Year 8		Autumn	Spring	Summer
		The Art of Rhetoric: From Aristotle to Modernity	Romeo and Juliet – a tragedy	Modernity: Pre- and Post-WW1 (OMaM)
	Intent	An exploration of the human identity, voice and the art of persuasion ranging from Aristotelian to modern and focusing on the use of ethos, pathos, logos. An extract-based unit studying the depth of speeches over time and across a range of cultures/identities, with the analysis of linked unseen non-fiction to further embed knowledge of key concepts.	An exploration of Shakespeare's classic tragedy, exploring key scenes throughout the play. An insight into William Shakespeare's life and Elizabethan and Jacobean England. A whole text study with in depth analysis of key scenes, and Shakespeare's use of language and structure to create sympathy, and its effect on a contemporary and modern day audience in order to support students in answering the question: Why is Shakespeare still relevant today?	A whole text study of Steinbeck's OMaM exploring the representation of minority identities and an overview of the human experience over time, with war poetry to develop ideas about society and how humans relate to nature.
	Key Concepts	Ethos, Pathos, Logos Argument Counter argument Audience as context	Tragedy Patriarchy Dramatic irony Foreshadowing Sonnet Monologue Soliloquy	Conflict Allusion Microcosm Society Cyclical
			1 x explicitly taught grammar lesson per week (final lesson)	1 x Reading for Pleasure lesson per week (final lesson)
	Mastering Writing	Vocab instruction: ethos, pathos, logos, anecdote, didactic, philosophy, antithesis, appositives, anaphora, Grammar: : 1st/2nd/3rd person pronouns, verbs, subject, construction of sentences: compound and complex, paragraphs, discourse markers, linking paragraphs.	Vocab instruction: tragic, prologue, sonnet, feud, status quo, obstacle, hyperbole, tragic flaw, exile, foreshadow, catastrophe Sustaining a thesis; structuring a thesis; future perfect continuous; non-defining relative clauses; defining relative clauses, balanced argument composure; correcting comma splices.	Vocabulary instruction: allegory, empower, ominous, unprecedented, volatile, isolation, segregation, hierarchy, foreshadowing. Minority. Grammar:
	Summative assessment	Pre- and post-unit cumulative knowledge check (MCQ) Non-fiction writing: writing to persuade	Pre- and post-unit cumulative knowledge check (MCQ) Reading assessment: How is the theme of love explored in Romeo and Juliet in Act 2 Scene 2? Inference, evidence, meaning.	Pre- and post-unit cumulative knowledge review (MCQ) Extract analysis – setting, inference, analysis, evidence.

FIGURE 3.2 *An example Year 8 English curriculum*

Year 9	Autumn	Spring	Summer
	Literary Anxiety: the Romantics and the Victorians	Image to Text	Diverse Voices: Language as a tool for social justice
Intent	A study of the presentation of childhood in Jane Eyre, and extracts from the likes of Poe, King, Dickens and Shelley that explore literature as a tool for examining the anxiety of the times. Thematically linked non-fiction and poems threaded throughout the unit to further develop key conceptual knowledge: Blake, Shelley, Coleridge, Byron.	A study of writing forms, audience and purpose and how best to be successful in their creation. Looking at examples of literary greats' use of conscious literary and structural devices, and teaching the skill of writing emulation.	A study of voices from the strands of diversity, ranging from poetry to novel extracts, looking at examples of how writers use language as a tool to advocate for social justice, to challenge prejudice and discrimination, and present identity through their words.
Key Concepts	Allusions Power of man/response to industrialisation and conflict Gender Place Archetypes Victorian attitudes	Narration and description Using language to paint a picture Show don't tell Written voice Perspective and viewpoint Conscious, linguistic crafting Emulation	Society Allusion Conflict Identity Advocacy Poetic Voice/Symbolism
Mastering Writing	Vocabulary instruction: dependent, to oppress, juxtaposition, thesis, to humiliate, hypocrite, comeuppance. Grammar: apostrophe of omission; the apostrophe; past perfect continuous; countable and uncountable nouns; future perfect simple; analytical verbs; thesis.	Vocabulary instruction: describe, narrate, structure, compel, convince, engage, character, perspective Grammar: tense consistency, ambiguity, shifts in focus, form and purpose, register and tone, dialogue integration, cohesion, sustained accuracy in subject verb agreement/singular and plural	Vocabulary instruction: diverse/diversity, oppression, social injustice, platform, social responsibility, equity, privilege Grammar: use of intonation when reading poetry aloud, evaluating and editing by proposing changes to vocabulary and grammar that enhance meaning, omission, appositive, form and structure, homophones, prefixes and suffixes
Summative assessment	Cumulative knowledge check (MCQ) Presentation of character analysis	Cumulative knowledge review (MCQ) Descriptive writing: emulation of writers' style to describe a world post-pandemic	Cumulative knowledge review (MCQ) Analysis of whole poem

1 x explicitly taught grammar lesson per week (final lesson)

1 x Reading for Pleasure lesson per week (final lesson)

FIGURE 3.3 *An example Year 9 English curriculum*

how they might want a curriculum to look, prior to taking middle leadership posts. This is all experience that will help you when, or if, you decide to climb the ladder towards curriculum leadership.

Lesson-planning

Lesson-planning can be as simple or as complex as you want it to be, but as we become more experienced and skilled practitioners, we can often use a stripped-back framework as a scaffold for the most pertinent areas to signpost.

The medium-term plan should be the guide to what goes into your lesson plans, as that way your lessons are planned as a sequence, linking to the prior and upcoming knowledge of the unit, rather than being a stand alone lesson which does not develop pupils' schema.

Lesson titles are useful for signposting the journey through the curriculum for the pupils as well as you. A clear title makes looking back for key knowledge easier to find, and later when pupils want to revise for assessments, makes that process much more accessible. The best titles are clear and precise, for example, 'What is an Epic hero?' or 'How is Oliver characterised?'

Cognitive science provides us with many clues as to how we learn most effectively: limitations of working memory, the testing effect, the forgetting curve, the impact of extraneous load; all of these, and more, are important to consider in lesson-planning so we can harness the 'best bets' for pupil learning. One of the most popular ways to do this is to follow Rosenshine's (2012) 'principles of instruction', which breaks lessons down into the following elements:

- daily review
- new material in small steps

- ask questions

- provide models

- guide student practice

- check student understanding

- obtain high success rate

- scaffolding for difficult tasks

- independent practice

- weekly and monthly review.

Of course, not all lessons will contain all of those elements, but a typical lesson might follow a format of:

- low-stakes quiz, retrieving prior knowledge relevant to this lesson

- review or check of this knowledge as formative assessment

- introduction of new material

- questioning of pupils on new material and links to prior knowledge

- teacher modelling of task

- pupils completing scaffolded task

- teacher checking for understanding and application.

This structure provides a solid foundation of cognitive science 'best bets', whilst also becoming a familiar routine which supports pupils' understanding and implementation of new and prior knowledge. It also removes the burden of thinking up whizzy and creative activities to fill pupils' time, as the focus is always on the teaching and learning of the core knowledge the curriculum is designed to impart.

Formative assessment

What do athletes and English students have in common?

A great deal, it would seem.

In *Making Good Progress?*, Daisy Christodoulou (2017b) writes: '[when] a physiotherapist designs a new stretching regime for a runner, they are deliberately choosing tasks that do not look like the final race for which the athlete is training [but are] also deliberately choosing tasks that they think will improve a particular aspect of the athlete's performance. The drill and the performance are different and separate, but they are linked.'

This is an apt comparison to make to the English classroom, despite many English teachers not being athletically minded, because the analogy is talking about formative assessment.

In simple terms, formative assessment monitors students' learning and provides feedback, whereas summative assessment is to evaluate the students' learning at the end of a unit.

For our athletes, the 'stretching regime' we are implementing before their final performance – the exam, and beyond – is where we ensure they have the skills and knowledge – broken down into its constituent parts, practised, re-taught, and practised again.

As teachers, we know when we're giving our formative assessment we must bear in mind that the sole focus of feedback should be to further pupils' progression through the curriculum. Feedback should empower pupils to take ownership for improving their work; adults should not be doing the work for the pupil. This is something that is sadly easy to get wrong. We've all experienced or heard horror stories of 'two stars and a wish'; 'triple marking'; or the fabled 'verbal feedback given' stamp. These are, patently, a poor use of our time.

And what's more, they aren't much use to our pupils either. Just like those athletes running their drills, what we provide our students with during the practice stage will have an impact in their final performance. What we need are precise and targeted assessment tasks.

So what might that look like? Well, let's consider a typical GCSE essay on *Macbeth* and the amount of information it provides to you as the teacher: plot knowledge, characterisation, context, analysis, quotation, paragraphing, discourse markers, spelling... the list goes on. How can we possibly infer from all this information what is a mistake, a misconception, or a lack of knowledge? It is just too vast and imprecise to be useful to us in moving pupils on. A mark scheme for a final essay – a summative assessment – is simply too scattergun for formative use when we need to be precise in ascertaining what needs to be re-taught, what the common misconceptions are and where gaps are.

Instead, what we need is something that can zoom in on the detail. What we need is a diagnostic task. These tasks are designed to bring to the attention of the teacher the areas where a student needs redirection or development. These tasks work within each scheme of learning as a much more useful way of making inferences about what we need to do.

A diagnostic task takes place once a reasonable period of learning has occurred – usually around two weeks, or six to seven lessons. Just like an athlete working on a particular aspect of their craft, it's not a 'cold task' as such because you'll spend a little time preparing – perhaps by using 'I do, we do' on a different part of a given extract, before the 'you do' is completed as a diagnostic task. Subsequent lessons should then look to prioritise two to three areas of weakness identified before retesting at the end of a unit. As a teacher, completing this task early in the unit allows you to personalise the journey towards the end point – the summative task.

Victorian Injustice: Year Ten Term One

Diagnostic Analysis Task:

How does Blake create a negative impression of London in the poem?

You may wish to consider:

- the language used.

- the form, structure, and rhyme scheme.

Remember to focus on how all of the evidence you choose creates a negative impression of London.

Complete this on your purple lined paper.

You will receive a whole-class feedback form to stick in when your teacher has read your work.

Final Assessment Task:

Before you complete this question on your orange paper, look back at your Diagnostic Task and the whole class feedback that you received.

What did you need to improve on? This extract is taken from the very end of the novel.

extract redacted for brevity

Starting with this extract, how does Dickens show the transformations of Scrooge's character in *A Christmas Carol*? Write about:

- how Dickens shows the transformation in this extract.

- how Dickens shows the transformation in the novel as a whole.

FIGURE 3.4 *Assessment task for the Year 10 unit,* 'A Christmas Carol: *Victorian injustice*'

This allows us to avoid 'exam factory' assessment – diagnostic tasks need not resemble the final assessment or practice exam question in terms of task or outcome. In fact, it may be more useful to produce a task which can be marked quickly but still allows you to make inferences about pupils' understanding as well as developing pupils' resilience to testing – see Figure 3.4 for an example from a Year 10 unit entitled '*A Christmas Carol*: Victorian injustice'.

Just like our athletes on the track looking over their performance times, what these tasks also do is allow us to focus explicitly on the smaller steps of progress. For our students, we can reflect on the progress made between the beginning and end of a topic or half term, and not how close pupils are to their 'end of Key Stage 4' target. This allows us to keep the 'dialogue' of previous targets going.

Ideally, the diagnostic and final tasks are the only formal written assessments in Years 7 to 10, and feedback is given via whole-class feedback sheets. For ease of tracking, you could ask students to complete tasks on different papers: for example, diagnostic tasks are completed on purple lined paper; final tasks are completed on orange lined paper. Feedback lessons where pupils address their targets in green pen should usually take place within six lessons. Feedback for the diagnostic assessments should *not* be given in the form of a mark or a grade, although teachers may note these for their own records. This is to allow pupils to focus on what they need to improve or develop, rather than fixating on a mark or grade. This is what true formative assessment means.

Summative assessment

Summative assessment is an assessment used to evaluate the pupils' learning at the end of a unit; it is formalised, usually high stakes and, to be accurate in its evaluations, should be normed across a wide sample.

In English, summative assessments are usually essay-based, likely because essay-writing provides so much information and tests so many skills: fluency, paragraphing, quotations, analysis, plot knowledge, context, characterisation, and so on, and it's in the tradition of the subject to write essays. Essays are marked using mark schemes that describe where pupils are right now rather than how to move them forward, and exam boards use them to sample and assess the whole domain (by domain here, we're talking about the curriculum), in a summative fashion, for as Daisy Christodoulou says, 'The domain that tests are trying to measure is the extent of a pupil's knowledge and skills and their ability to apply these skills in the real world in the future. The domain is vast, and normally we have just a two or three hour exam to try and measure this domain' (2017b).

The exam boards use summative assessments which are carefully designed not just to test what's on the exam, but to use that as a deduction of students' knowledge of the aspects of the domain covered in the curriculum (or specification) but not in the exam. With carefully designed questions, these inferences are valid and reliable. When the marking is moderated and the results are normed, this allows for relatively fair and accurate evaluations of pupils' knowledge, and for shared meaning of outcome to be created in the form of grades.

When we use summative assessments in schools, we are usually using them formatively, that is, we do something with that information, using it to identify where common misconceptions are, what has not been understood, what has not been taught effectively, what needs re teaching, and so on. And because summative assessments are not designed to be used formatively, they are not usually the best means of finding this information out. For most of us, formative assessment strategies are our most useful tools of assessment.

Next steps for assessment planning

- Check the assessment calendar for data points and map back so you have time to assess, mark and input data.
- Consult your long-term knowledge planning to check which knowledge you want retained over time, and that you therefore need to assess.
- Consider the most effective assessment for the knowledge: MCQs for substantive knowledge? Short-answer questions for procedural knowledge? Labelling of examples? Consider how longer written answers, if any, will be assessed/marked.
- Build in time to look at patterns and trends from the assessment and use these to inform re-teaching and future curriculum planning.

Summary

- Assessment should enable reflective teaching.
- Powerful knowledge is key.
- The curriculum is the progression model.
- Curriculum content should allow students to broaden their minds, and to see the world through other lenses.
- Only assess what has been taught.

4

The importance
of literature

Mary Hind-Portley and Fe Brewer

Introduction

Humans are wired for story. 'Story is what the brain does,' says journalist Will Storr (2019). John Sutherland (2013), a professor of Modern English Literature, writes that 'literature is the human mind at the very height of its ability to express and interpret the world around us. Literature... does not simplify, but it enlarges our minds and sensibilities to the point where we can better handle complexity... it makes us more human.' Therefore, story should be at the heart of our English curriculum, helping our students to read widely and analytically, and also to develop their ability to create story. A starting point is the National Curriculum for considering literature in your curriculum.

The National Curriculum outlines what teachers are expected to include in their curricula: 'Reading at Key Stage 3 should be wide, varied and challenging. Pupils should be expected to read whole books, to read in depth and to read for pleasure and information.' This is then specified in greater detail:

Pupils should be taught to:

- *develop an appreciation and love of reading, and read increasingly challenging material independently through:*
  - ○ *reading a wide range of fiction and non-fiction, including in particular whole books, short stories, poems and plays with a wide coverage of genres, historical periods, forms and authors. The range will include high-quality works from:*
    - ■ *English literature, both pre-1914 and contemporary, including prose, poetry and drama*
    - ■ *Shakespeare (two plays)*
    - ■ *seminal world literature*
  - ○ *choosing and reading books independently for challenge, interest and enjoyment*
  - ○ *re-reading books encountered earlier to increase familiarity with them and provide a basis for making comparisons.*

Department for Education (2013)

Literature, then, is a significant part of our curriculum and it is worth discussing this within your department, particularly if some team members come from a language or linguistics background. The term 'literature' itself can be contentious, as it can be interpreted in different ways, for example, 'Literature' with a capital 'L', as in texts from the Western literary canon. However, literature should be understood in its broadest term and we should consider how we approach a breadth of literature representative of a range of cultures.

It is very healthy to discuss and debate the literature you wish your students to experience. You may find it useful to consider the development of literature over time before planning or updating your English curriculum. Some schools do focus on a simple chronology in Year 7 to help contextualise later reading, but this is just one approach. By considering the chronology of Western literature, we can then decide which aspects of this we wish to include in our curriculum, perhaps through anthologising texts and extracts, or to decide which texts we think are important for our students to experience. Alongside the Western canon, it is also important to consider canonical texts from across the world and to engage with those who have expert knowledge of these.

Reflecting on English literature in your curriculum

In this section, we will outline the main literary periods and movements, but first here are some questions to support the curriculum-planning process or to support reflections about your current curriculum.

Prompt questions

- What do we know about this literary period?
- Who has expertise on this within the department?
- What further research or CPD do we need to undertake?
- Which texts from this period may we want to include in our curriculum and why?
- How will these texts develop our students' experience and understanding of literature? Why do they need this experience?

The following sections are simple overviews of English literary periods and movements to prompt further reading and research. There is a growing body of research on decolonising and diversifying the curriculum, such as Bennie Kara's *A Little Guide for Teachers: Diversity in Schools* (2020) as well as Low and Wynne-Davies' *A Black British Canon?* (2006). In addition, the TED Talk, 'The danger of a single story', by Chimamanda Ngozi Adichie (2009) is a useful starting point. It is important to discuss this further in your department and consult those who are experts. This section of our book aims to offer a summary of the main British literary movements, but acknowledges those voices who are absent from this.

Origins of the Western literary tradition – Ancient Greece and earlier

We could begin with the *Epic of Gilgamesh*, an epic carved on stone, written in Sumerian. It is interesting, as teachers, to consider how this connects with aetiological stories from around the world. We can certainly make connections with Greek myths and the Bible. Let us then consider the significance of the Ancient Greeks and their influence on the Western canon. If we simplify this into myths, drama and rhetoric, we can make links from these three categories to our modern English curricula. The influence of Greek myths, and indeed Roman myths, can be traced in the work of many dramatists, poets and novelists, particularly Renaissance writers who experienced a 'classical' education. To support our students studying Shakespeare, the 'Romantics' and nineteenth-century novels and much other writing, knowledge of a range of Greek myths will help their ability to infer from and understand classical allusions. Now you may wish to decide which aspects of Greek literature to include in your curriculum.

Myths

There are numerous versions of Greek myths to choose from and it is worth considering which versions or translations you will use, as each version has a particular view of the myth they are retelling. This website is a very helpful starting point:

https://classictales.educ.cam.ac.uk, as is the work of Dr Arlene Holmes-Henderson, and the Classics for All organisation. It is also worth considering what pupils have learnt about Greek myths in Key Stage 2, and the opportunities they are given to recall and apply their knowledge in Key Stage 3.

One notable aspect about this period is the oral tradition characterised by epic and lyric poetry such as *The Iliad* and *The Odyssey*, attributed to Homer. You may wish to consider whether retellings written specifically for children are to be a part of your curriculum or your own reading, or whether you'll be using extracts from modern translations. What can pupils learn from these which supports their development as readers and writers? How do Greek myths and other myths influence screenwriters? When we discuss cultural capital, Greek literature is one key aspect of this!

Drama

Is there a place for exploring Greek drama in our English curricula? Does your drama department teach Greek drama? What links could you make with them? The conventions of Greek drama influence and underpin many of the plays we may study in KS3 and KS4, so it seems logical that we consider a play in KS3. From this study, pupils would understand the origins of Western drama and its conventions. Linking this to ideas from Plato's *Poetics* introduces them to a theory of drama which supports the study of plays from the sixteenth century onwards. This also supports students in studying the art of rhetoric and helps them to explore further Greek myths.

Rhetoric

While we may be more used to exploring rhetoric linked to writing, we have placed it here to consider how Graeco-Roman rhetoric has influenced both drama, poetry and prose.

Texts to consider

- *The Epic of Gilgamesh* (Ancient Sumeria)
- Homer's *The Iliad* and *The Odyssey*
- Aeschylus's *Prometheus Bound*
- Ovid's *Metamorphoses*

Note: Texts presented in these lists are primarily for staff to consider reading. Some you may wish to consider as curriculum choices.

Anglo-Saxon and Norse literature

Now we move on in both time and location to the time circa 450 to 1066, once again considering the oral tradition. The British Library carries an interesting collection of surviving Anglo-Saxon texts. Many of the surviving literary texts are anonymous, such as *Beowulf*; however, two named writers are Caedmon and Cynewulf. While *Beowulf* is a well-known text now, it was relatively unknown until 1815, when a transcript was published by a Danish scholar, Thorkelin. *Beowulf* is a significant text as it shows us the rich tradition of heroic poetry following the settlement of Germanic peoples in England. The period is also interesting because of the confluence of Germanic languages with Latin as the pre-Christian world merges with the Christian world through the influence of Latin. Surviving texts are in both Old English (the vernacular) and Latin. If you teach students who show significant interest in this time period and who might want to study this later, the University of Cambridge offers a fascinating undergraduate degree in Anglo-Saxon, Norse and Celtic, which explores many aspects of this fascinating period in history.

Texts to consider

- Kevin Crossley-Holland's *The Anglo-Saxon World: An Anthology*
- *Beowulf* translated by Seamus Heaney
- *The Battle of Maldon*

Middle English and medieval literature

If we take the famous date of 1066 as the beginning of this period, we can then consider the influence of the Normans on the continuing development of language and literature. However, many years pass by until we can see the influences on writing emerging. This period has many surviving administrative, religious and political texts, which enable us to track the changes from Old to Middle English, where Middle English becomes ever closer to the language we recognise today. One interesting exercise with pupils is to place copies of the *Lord's Prayer* (the *Our Father*) in chronological order to help them understand how our language has changed over time. *The Story of English* by Professor David Crystal (2005), an expert on the English language and much more, can provide insightful contextual knowledge of language development which can support both classroom study of medieval literature, and also vocabulary and language change. This and Crystal's other works are invaluable for learning more about English language and literature as teachers.

For those who could not read, access to literature was through wall paintings, sculptures and listening to works read aloud as a communal experience (aurality). People were also surrounded by carvings of literary works. The silent, private experience of reading was afforded to only a few. It is interesting to consider how this affected the telling and reception of stories. Knowing your work may be enacted as a tapestry must have influenced the process of production. Paintings in churches were one way biblical stories were shared with worshippers; some of these wall paintings have survived the Reformation so we are able to consider how these were encountered.

In addition, mystery plays and other performances formed part of the medieval experience of literature beyond the written word.

Sir Gawain and the Green Knight is a significant text, written around 1400, describing the adventures of Gawain, a nephew of King Arthur. The text came into the possession of Sir Robert Cotton who owned a copy of *Beowulf* and *The Lindisfarne Gospels*. *Sir Gawain* did not reappear until Victorian times. The text is now stored in the British Library with images available on their website (see the 'Discovering Literature' section). The translation by Simon Armitage does make this accessible for pupils and this (or certainly extracts from it) could be read as part of an anthology with students looking at the development of storytelling over time. The disruption of the equilibrium of the court of King Arthur by a mysterious figure resonates with our understanding of the art and conventions of story structure. This then prepares for further tales of knights' adventures and the concept of chivalry.

Thomas Malory's *Le Morte Darthur* (circa 1470), charting the rise and fall of King Arthur, is a fitting text to consider here. This work is regarded as one of the greatest explorations of chivalry and the triplet of courtesy, duty and obligation. It also, however, explores the darker side of this world. Indeed, Malory's own life is a tale of this dark world too. *Le Morte Darthur* is the last work to recount the Arthurian legend and the only work to cover the whole of the legend, from King Arthur's birth to his death. The invention of the printing press by William Caxton is a further significant event in the Middle Ages as it has secured us access to texts of this time.

There are many more important texts in this literary period, such as Chaucer's *The Canterbury Tales*, and the British Library site is an excellent gateway to further reading (see www.bl.uk/medieval-literature/works).

Texts to consider

For the classroom:

- *Sir Gawain and the Green Knight* translated by Simon Armitage
- Thomas Malory's *Le Morte Darthur*
- Geoffrey Chaucer's *The Canterbury Tales*

Other works worth exploring to support your knowledge of the period:

- William Langland's *Piers Plowman*
- *The Owl and the Nightingale*

Early modern and the Renaissance

This period has been described by Hiscock and Wilcox (2017) as 'one of the greatest periods of writing in English – a strikingly fertile age of literary innovation and creativity'. The end of the War of the Roses, the rise of the Tudors and the influence of the printing press contribute to an interesting and exciting time for the development of literature. The debates and tensions around religion and political power, the rise of humanism, and the changes in readership led to a desire to widen intellectual horizons. Here, we find our famous names and perhaps texts and writers which feel more like common ground.

While we may now be unfamiliar with the vernacular English of the time, it is important that this original language is explored with our students and that we build their confidence to access these texts. How can we familiarise ourselves with this period? Firstly, we can look at the major poets, in particular, Edmund Spenser. His verse epic *The Faerie Queene* (1590) is a significant text in this period. It continues the tradition of the knight undergoing a journey; indeed, it focuses on a number of medieval knights. Spenser writes in a deliberately archaic style, drawing on myth and history. We can look back to the tales of King Arthur and our earlier text *Le Morte Darthur*. *The Faerie Queene* makes us consider the importance of allegory in literature, as each book follows the adventures of a knight who represents a particular virtue (holiness, temperance, chastity, friendship, justice and courtesy) and who has that quality in him or herself tested by the plot. Spenser explores the Elizabethan idea of virtue, written in honour of Elizabeth I. The work demands that we have knowledge of Elizabethan politics and history. Spenser's work is both a critique and celebration of the Tudors, particularly religious reforms. Spenser wanted the poem to 'fashion a gentleman or noble person in virtuous and gentle disciple'. The verse form invented by Spenser is known as the Spenserian stanza.

Whilst many changes were taking place in literature, this period also marked a return to the importance of classical literature and culture through the grammar school system. The influence of Greek and Latin texts can be seen in the works of the major writers of the period. It is interesting to consider the influence of Ovid's *Metamorphoses* on Shakespeare, as well as Aristotle's *Poetics*. The theatre began to flourish and alongside Shakespeare, we have the work of Christopher Marlowe, Ben Jonson and John Webster. It is also right that we recognise that there are many absent voices, particularly female ones. Including an overarching 'big question' in KS3, such as 'Whose voices do we hear and whose voices do we not hear?', supports an ongoing enquiry into representation in the literary canon. It is useful to discuss this with history colleagues also. For example, Catherine Parr was a religious writer, not just the sixth wife of Henry VIII.

Texts to consider

- Edmund Spenser's *The Faerie Queene*
- A selection of Shakespeare's plays
- Christopher Marlowe's *Dr Faustus*
- Ben Jonson's *Volpone*
- John Webster's *The Duchess of Malfi*

The seventeenth century and the Restoration

As the Caroline era begins when Charles I comes to the throne in 1625, and some of the great names of the sixteenth century die, we move into a time when the divine right of kings is questioned, and parliament seeks to curb the power of the monarchy. This is a period of disturbance and challenge, with the Civil War, followed by the Restoration. During this time, the rise of Cromwell and the Puritans led to the closure of the theatre.

We can look at works of poetry such as those by John Donne and the rise of the Metaphysical poets. Donne's poems *The Flea* and *A Valediction* are two famous examples of his work. He explores emotions in great depth, such as joy and death, shame and pain. His poetry is characterised by jarring rhythms, and rich and contradictory metaphors. While the metaphysical tradition wasn't a cohesive movement, we can also consider the poets Thomas Carew, Henry Vaughan and Andrew Marvell as well.

Another significant poet is John Milton, creator of the epic poem *Paradise Lost*. Milton's list of writing is long and diverse, but he spent his life wrestling with ideas of religious, political and personal freedom in the context of different forms of governance by the Church and state. When we trace the line of influence and intertextuality across time, we see the complexity of these influences in Milton's poem. This is a fascinating work to read as teachers as it challenges us with its classical and religious allusions. We can link back to Shakespeare and the arc of epic and tragedy from Ancient Greek literature.

Many, now typical and familiar literary forms, such as the novel, biography, history, travel-writing and journalism, developed during the Restoration period.

Once the monarchy is restored and the theatres re-open, we see the range of playwrights at work and the development of what is now termed Restoration Comedy, which Diane Maybank (2018) describes as 'a comic vision that ridiculed what it most admired'. We see both female playwrights and women taking roles on the stage much more publicly. We also see a growing diversity in theatre audiences. Maybank comments that 'Restoration comedies have faced many obstacles in their 350-year journey to the modern stage. Throughout the eighteenth century, scripts were subject to heavy revisions and bowdlerisation. By the nineteenth century, the plays were considered highly immoral, artificial or just plain old-fashioned.' However, when we consider them in their context, we understand why the plays were written in a particular style. When looking at plays to read and study in Key Stage 3, would we consider a Restoration comedy?

Texts to consider

- Aphra Behn's *The Rover*
- John Donne's *The Major Works*
- John Milton's *Paradise Lost*

The eighteenth century

This period can be divided into different eras, such as the Augustan era, which refers to the Roman Emperor Augustus who presided over the golden age of Roman literature. The fashion of writing was to imitate refined Greek and Latin classical models. This imitation came to be known as neoclassicism. Alexander Pope is a significant writer of the time, notable for works such as *The Rape of the Lock* and *An Essay on Criticism*, as well as his translations of *The Iliad* and *The Odyssey*.

A later dominant figure is that of Samuel Johnson, 'arguably the most distinguished man of letters in English history' (according to the Oxford Dictionary of National Biography) and writer of, amongst other things, the first English dictionary. He had an eclectic career and we benefit from his literary criticism, travel-writing and biography. It is worth considering how examples of his work could be used in Key Stage 3 as they lend themselves to different units of work, and show students the forerunner of modern biography and travel-writing.

The British Library's 'Discovering Literature' pages show us the diversity of writers at work during this time. We see the rise of the novelist too, with works such as *Tristram Shandy*, which plays with conventions and metafictionality. We also have Margaret Cavendish and her very early example of science fiction, *The Blazing World.* This woman-centric novel explores a created world, reached via the North Pole, which is populated by mostly anthropomorphised animals. The central character is shipwrecked there and becomes their ruler. The story follows the survival of 'the young Lady onely, by the light of her Beauty, the heat of her Youth, and Protection of the Gods, remaining alive'. It is interesting to explore the immediate acceptance of the 'Lady' as their ruler, alongside the story world Cavendish creates. Students could discuss the elements now common to science fiction and fantasy genres which Cavendish employs. They could also explore the use of Greek mythology in the story as well. This could form part of a unit of work on science fiction and fantasy through the ages.

Overall, this is a fascinating period of literary development and one which is often overlooked in curriculum-planning. Perhaps it deserves further exploration.

Texts to consider

- Margaret Cavendish's *The Blazing World*
- *Letters of the Late Ignatius Sancho, an African*
- Jonathan Swift's *Gulliver's Travels*

The nineteenth century

This nineteenth century continued to see an evolution in literature which reflected the rapid changes in society and technology. More than any previous century, literature evolved in many directions as copyright laws and printing technology evolved, and literacy rates rose. No longer was literature the preserve of educated upper and middle classes; by the mid-1800s almost anyone could access literature, and the market responded accordingly. While Thackeray and Scott novels sold plentifully to those who enjoyed a solid three-volume novel, less 'refined' literature offered satisfaction to those with more bawdy taste. For examples, so-called 'penny dreadfuls' (crude stories about vicious crimes and scandalous behaviour) could be picked up cheaply and plentifully.

Many nineteenth-century writers opted to follow French literary trends and adopted realism, focusing on the lives of ordinary people in ordinary places. George Eliot and the Brontë sisters depicted the lives and locations they knew, with people who held ordinary desires and aspirations, albeit extraordinary lives. This continued through the century and can be seen beautifully in Thomas Hardy's novels which, set in Wessex, follow the adventures of characters with often modest means and ambitions.

On the other end of the spectrum, Gothic literature became a popular genre twice during the century and explored themes of science, religion and morality which echoed contemporary thinking and how traditionally accepted ideas and orders were increasingly being challenged. Yet, almost simultaneously, Jane Austen's novels reveal that there were many in society for whom eerie castles and challenges to God's power were far from desirable ways to occupy one's mind.

Many writers also used fiction as a platform for social or moral campaigns, most notably Charles Dickens. Utilising the literature market as a vessel for moral messages (and as a good source of cash), his writing often highlighted the corruption of social and religion institutions, earning him a place in the nation's hearts and his very own adjective – 'Dickensian'. Many other writers followed the trends set by Dickens, particularly when setting their writing in London, acknowledging and utilising the many faces of the world's largest city: Robert Louis Stevenson, Arthur Conan Doyle, Arthur Morrison, Marie Corelli, Oscar Wilde and many others.

Plays were also highly popular. While many echoed the realism often found in the novels of the time (such as works by Henrik Ibsen and Anton Chekhov) or were rushed adaptations of popular works, the theatre also echoed the era's love of satire (such as Oscar Wilde's comedies). Poetry was also varied and popular throughout the era as another form to explore the new and changing world.

Texts to consider

- Arthur Conan-Doyle's *The Tales of Sherlock Holmes*
- Edgar Allen Poe's *The Raven*
- Christina Rossetti's poetry
- Oscar Wilde's *The Happy Prince and Other Tales*

The twentieth century

Now we are much closer to our present day and we consider a period of time marked by two world wars. Writers in the Edwardian era often sought to explore social and political change in both prose and drama, exploring and challenging the shortcomings of society. The website crossref-it.info provides a series of articles which summarise aspects of the twentieth century pertaining to literature.

We can consider how this time period is divided into the Edwardian and pre-World War I period, World War I, the interwar period, World War II, and the post-war period. Writers commonly explored the significance of the class system and how this was challenged by the impact of the world wars. The changing fortunes of the British Empire also had a significant influence on literature. It's also worth exploring the rise of Modernism and the influence of American writers, such as T. S. Eliot, on English literature and the impact of Celtic modernism, such as James Joyce's *Ulysses* and W. B. Yeats's works. The rise of the Bloomsbury group is also notable, with works such as Virginia Woolf's *A Room of One's Own*.

The economic collapse of the 1920s and 1930s and the rise of fascism led to a bleak outlook in fiction and non-fiction. Furthermore, the dispersal of people and rationing seem to have affected literary output and production; paper was rationed for one thing. A focus on the lives of the working classes arises, with such classics as Walter Greenwood's *Love on the Dole*, which can be linked with George Orwell's *The Road to Wigan Pier*. Graham Greene's *Brighton Rock* explores desperate loneliness. The key words seem to be despair and defiance in interwar literature. Writers also begin to challenge and explore sexual repression, particularly the repression of homosexuality during the Second World War.

Post-war religion and allegory seem to appear as themes in writing from interwar writers, in contrast with the emerging writing of 'The Angry Young Men', their quasi-documentary style of fiction cataloguing their desire for social mobility. Amongst these are John Osborne's *Look Back in Anger* and Alan Sillitoe's *Saturday Night, Sunday Morning*. While not included in the label, angry young women such as Doris Lessing and Shelagh Delaney also became prominent. Post-colonial writing develops from Paul Scott to Salman Rushdie and Vikram Seth, all very different in their exploration of post-colonial society. While it seems that male writers are prominent above, female writers such as Muriel Spark, Iris Murdoch and Agatha Christie explored class, the roles of men and women, and sexuality. This leads us to those feminist writers who used the fairy tale and the Gothic to explore their ideas about society, such as Angela Carter and Jeannette Winterson.

It is at this point that the summary we offer here cannot cover the output of the latter end of the twentieth century and we encourage you to continue to research the sweep of English literary traditions, constantly expanding your learning and horizons. Also, our curriculum time is precious and we cannot cover all of the literary periods above in depth, so our text choices need to be robust enough to carry the weight of their traditions and to help students see how generations of writers are influenced by or rebel against the traditions which have preceded them.

Seminal world literature

The Western canon is just one of many. As mentioned on page 80, the English National Curriculum asks us to 'develop an appreciation and love of reading, and read increasingly challenging material independently' through a number of different text types, including 'seminal world literature'.

However, no guidance has been given as to what 'seminal world literature' might mean. The very phrase directly implies a judgement; however, this also gives us freedom to choose what we consider to be seminal world texts. When you are selecting texts, consider the following points:

- How does the literature we choose represent our cohorts?

- How do our choices open up our cohorts to a world beyond their own?

- How expert are we in teaching literature from around the world?

- Why are the texts we have chosen significant both in their culture and globally?

Texts to consider

- Chinua Achebe's *Things Fall Apart*
- Kazuo Ishiguro's *Never Let Me Go*
- Marjane Satrapi's *Persepolis*

Children's literature

While it is the first literature our students ever experience, children's literature is – arguably – a relatively modern phenomenon. The very existence of the genre itself reflects changing concepts of childhood during the eighteenth and nineteenth centuries when our modern ideas of childhood developed along with laws against child labour and the introduction of compulsory education. In the same era, the expansion of the middle classes and technological developments in printing allowed for the creation of a brand-new market: children.

Of course, that's not to say that children were never taught stories before that. Oral tales have been used to socialise, advise and guide young people for many thousands of years, but from the eighteenth century onwards, these slowly and steadily evolved into now-familiar fairy tales which were designed explicitly for children, either to charm or educate them, and often both. Beginning with the translation of fairy tales from the continent by the Grimm Brothers and Hans Christian Andersen, children's literature established a strong market and – much like adult literature – boomed as literacy rates rose and printing became cheaper. For the first time, writers such as Edith Nesbit, Andrew Lang and Kenneth Grahame found themselves being cast by publishers as writers exclusively of children's literature (which did not always comply with their wishes). By the early twentieth century, children's literature had evolved into a multi-faceted genre providing a wealth of works, from illustrated story books for younger children to longer stories and novels for pre-teens, such as those by Enid Blyton and Arthur Ransome.

Fast forward to today, and children's literature is worth over £700 million a year in the UK alone and it continues to both reflect and shape our changing world. Series of books such as the Harry Potter novels and *Diary of a Wimpy Kid* have staggering popularity that transcends the books they began as, revealing the strength of the market. Many children's novels also remain true to the original purpose of children's literature: to instil a strong moral compass within children and give them safe exposure to the difficulties of the world. Some depict the experience of refugees, violent crime, different ethnic communities, mental health and challenging periods in our history. Illustrated stories and graphic novels sometimes serve the same purpose – despite their seemingly innocent form – and books such as Armin Greder's *The Island* and Eoin Colfer and Andrew Donkin's *Illegal* are rich sources of discussion about topical issues, while books such as Wolf Eribruch's *Death, Duck and the Tulip* can offer us perspectives on life. Moreover, the industry is – thankfully – increasingly recognising the need for all children to see themselves portrayed in the stories they read and to read literature from a diverse range of voices.

Why would we use children's literature in our curriculum then? Given the purpose of children's literature, it allows us to explore the ideals that society wants to portray (such as the focus on knights and King Arthur, particularly in the Victorian and Edwardian era), or the concepts it wants children to understand (consider the books about anxiety published during the Covid-19 pandemic). As such, it allows us to clearly explore literature as a construct and a vessel for moral or social messages.

Texts to consider

- George Cruikshank's *The Fairy Library*
- Frances Hodgson-Burnett's *The Secret Garden*
- C. S. Lewis's *The Lion, The Witch and The Wardrobe*
- Ruta Sepetys's *Between Shades of Grey*
- Alex Wheatle's *Cane Warriors*
- Patrice Lawrence's *Orangeboy*
- Chinua Achebe's *Chike and the River*

Play texts

Ask any group of students which came first – novels, poetry or plays – and they'll almost certainly say novels. The widespread availability of the form these days means that, while plays and spoken poetry are a far older form, students' experience of literature is largely rendered in extended prose. While this isn't a problem per se, it can be problematic when we explore play texts in our classrooms because, in being designed for live performance (bar a very select few such as Ibsen's *Peer Gynt*), they operate within a different set of rules.

They also have their own history and evolution which, by necessity when we have a finite amount of curriculum time, are rarely explored in our classrooms, but have significant implications for their meanings. Unlike the new genres introduced in prose literature (which is, of course, much younger), several theatrical genres are thousands of years old, namely comedy, tragedy and satire. Having been forged in the amphitheatres of Ancient Greece, these genres have been defined with structures, tropes and archetypes by Aristotle, then Shakespeare, and then challenged and reshaped by modern playwrights. As such, when we examine the structures and archetypes of play texts, we must consider the journey these have been on and the reasons behind each playwright's chosen nuances.

As well as the structures and characters of plays changing, the theatrical methods and performance values of play texts have changed dramatically, particularly over the past 200 years. For example, stage directions – something entirely unique to the form – have been not only influenced by changing dramatic styles and conventions, but also by technological and architectural advances. Stage directions in Renaissance plays are minimal and functional: 'he falls', 'exeunt, pursued by bear'. In contrast, from the mid-nineteenth century onwards, stage directions sometimes come with extraordinary detail: set designs, notes on actors' movements, facial expressions and gestures. Sound effects and lighting directions are sometimes detailed too, reflecting the availability of technology that Shakespeare and his contemporaries couldn't even conceive; imagine following Ibsen or Priestley's detailed set designs, prop demands and lighting effects in an Elizabethan theatre open to the elements.

We could easily, as English teachers, ignore the complex demands of plays and resort to exploring them as we would prose – language analysis with plot, theme and character exploration – but to do so would be to neglect their form and narrow their meaning. And when they offer such a rich history, why would we?

Texts to consider

- Shelagh Delaney's *A Taste of Honey*
- Christopher Marlowe's *Doctor Faustus*
- Henrik Ibsen's *Ghosts*
- Sophocles's *Oedipus Rex*
- Tony Kushner's *Angels in America*
- Ambreen Razia's *Diary of a Hounslow Girl*

Summary

- Continue to develop individual and collective knowledge about literary time periods, their usefulness and their limitations, using the suggested reading above. How can we identify what we do not know?
- Question who is represented and who is not – and consider what we need to learn about unrepresented voices.
- Consider how we help students to recognise the significance of a text 'in time' and also how current readings of the text influence our interpretations, for example, using extracts from critical reading.

5

Writing in English

*Laura Tsabet, Holly Wimbush, Abigail Mann,
Zara Shah, Davina Canham and
Laura May Rowlands*

Introduction

Aside from reading, writing is perhaps one of the most challenging skills that we learn. It can be daunting, not only technically, but emotionally too. To put thought and feeling onto paper is to give it permanence in a way that simply saying it does not. It is an expression of self, feelings and beliefs that many of us find therapeutic, enjoyable and rewarding, yet there are still many who do not find this solace in writing and see little value in it.

As English teachers, our job is to teach writing in a way that inspires our pupils, showing them how enlightening, thought-provoking and gratifying writing can be; all this whilst trying to navigate the curriculum and prepare pupils for exams which, some argue, stifle creativity. This is no mean feat and sometimes can feel like an incredible weight to bear, particularly for those of us who are sensitive to the struggles pupils may face if they leave school without having mastered this invaluable skill.

This chapter provides strategies to help support the teaching of writing in the classroom. It is by no means an exhaustive list and goes hand in hand with many fantastic books which already exist on this subject.

Research and theory

Despite the difficulties faced by many school children due to the Covid-19 pandemic, the National Literacy Trust report dated June 2020 (Clark et al.) showed a four per cent increase in the number of children who claimed to enjoy writing in their free time. Moreover, the number of children who said that they wrote outside of the classroom increased to 21.5 per cent in 2020, up from 16.5 per cent the year before (although significantly lower than the 27 per cent a decade previously). While it is obviously good news that some pupils have picked up their pens again and are using writing as a means of expressing themselves creatively or to support their own wellbeing, this is still very much the minority of our country's young people, and these figures could in fact have been the direct result of children spending more time at home with very little else to do during a national lockdown.

The National Literacy Trust report also showed that more girls than boys were writing outside of the classroom and cited their writing as being for enjoyment. This is largely in line with much of the research into children and young people's writing. Evidence collated by the Department for Education in their report, 'What is the research evidence on writing?' (2012), indicates that there is a gender gap in pupils' performance in writing, with girls outperforming boys throughout the key stages – a phenomenon which many experienced teachers will already be very familiar with.

Interestingly, the Department for Education report also highlighted how pupils' confidence in their ability to write well decreased as they got older, with Key Stage 4 pupils less likely to say that they were very good writers than in lower key stages. As secondary English teachers, we must ask ourselves why this is. What is it about writing at GCSE that is causing them to lose confidence? Is their capacity to be fully creative stifled by time constraints and mark schemes perhaps, or is it that they feel as though the quality of their writing is being judged against GCSE gradings before they've even finished the course?

To answer these questions, it is important that we start at the very beginning, when the mechanics of writing begins with the teaching of grammar. According to the EEF (2019a), various evaluations have determined that grammar interventions can have a positive impact on writing; however, the route to this approach may vary. Debra Myhill's extensive work in the field, in collaboration with Pearson, insists that 'Grammar for Writing' must be taught in context (see Jones et al., 2012), whereas Christodoulou promotes 'decontextualised drill', which then requires whole-school embedding (Didau, 2014). Regardless of the route, taking heed from one of the founders of the cognitive linguistics movement and the creator of cognitive grammar, Ronald Langacker (1987), might resolve some of the challenges we face and re instil this lost confidence in our pupils. Langacker proposes a cognitive approach to the development of writing that connects syntax with symbolism and semantics as if they are on a continuum, where grammar is deconstructed into patterns to represent concepts. Understanding and considering this approach might be just what we need to overcome the cognitive constraints of writing and to support our pupils with automation in the writing process.

Putting it into practice

Word classes

'Learning to write is about learning to be powerful' Debra Myhill (2014)

To wield this power, we rely on knowledge. The knowledge of individual constituents that come together in different forms, taking shape, constructing meaning, and giving our thoughts and expression both agency and power. To construct expression with power, expression that moves, expression that impacts, expression that makes someone pause and reflect or expression that inspires and ignites, we need to know what it is that we are wielding; we need to appreciate the magic of the individual word and its many guises.

Word: the smallest, relatively independent carrier of meaning. A construct that has acoustic and semantic identity. A construct that has morphological stability and syntactic mobility. We only need to re-read Imtiaz Dharker's poem 'The Right Word' or revisit Wilfred Owen's drafts of 'Dulce et Decorum Est' to appreciate this and to appreciate the semantic nuances between the choices that we make: is it 'freedom fighter' or is it 'guerrilla warrior'? Is it 'gargling' or is it 'guttering'? Does it matter? We know it does.

And this is why the knowledge of word classes matters. The ability to deconstruct an expression into its derivative components is as important as the ability to build it up again, brick by brick. While we may not have adequate time to do cognitive grammar the justice that it deserves, we can, and should, teach grammar explicitly to ensure that our pupils can wield this power for themselves.

The good news is that pupils have a foundation in place for grammar, established in primary school; the metalanguage has been foregrounded, and is continually reinforced during the teaching of modern foreign languages. Our focus, therefore, should be on revisiting and building on this existing knowledge base to enrich their schemas and commit prior knowledge to long-term memory. Here are some key areas that we can use as pivots.

Concrete and abstract nouns

Show pupils the power of manipulation and conscious crafting by combining concrete and abstract concepts in a sentence. For example:

She swallowed the beans (concrete noun) and her pride (abstract noun).

Note: when written in this coordinated form, this technique is also called zeugma.

Noun phrases

Teach the following word classes to demonstrate how we can expand noun phrases to enrich descriptions:

Determiner + adverb + adjective + noun + prepositional phrase

For example:

An + unusually + large + man + with heavy, broad shoulders.

Take this further by demonstrating what happens when we manipulate the word classes in this construct; swap the determiner 'an' with definite article 'the', or the concrete noun 'man' with, 'silhouette'. Encourage the repositioning of modifiers. When pupils know what modifiers are, syntactic manipulation can be taught easily and its dramatic impact appreciated. Changing the construct to 'The man, unusually large, with heavy, broad shoulders' makes the crafting both imaginative and exciting.

Verbs

Verbs manipulate tone and mood, and pupils need explicit instruction on how this is achieved. Notice the dynamic verbs in the following sentence from Charlie Higson's *Hurricane Gold*:

'There was a cacophony of different sounds; crashing, hissing, roaring, squealing, rumbling.'

These verbs create immediacy, tension, urgency and chaos, and in their present participle form are even more dramatic. Let pupils exercise creativity by changing the tone of the description through verbs. What happens if the verbs describe movement instead of sound? What happens if the verbs are only dynamic or stative? The opening and closing extracts in *Of Mice and Men* can be used as effective models to support this activity.

It is important to note that ongoing review is essential to secure understanding and transfer of the metalanguage of word classes to long-term memory. Only then can pupils confidently access grammatical knowledge structures relevant to task and context, and subsequently become every English teacher's dream: 'conscious' crafters.

Powerful sentences

Constructing a powerful sentence is the foundation of our expression, whether that is via academic or creative writing. Pupils must value their own voice when discussing literary works; they must see themselves as literary critics. We can support their development by slowing down the process of writing and almost micro-teaching elements of essay-writing to have a bigger impact.

With the formulaic structure of an exam question, the word 'presented' has been included in many exam-style questions over the years and it can be supremely limiting to pupils. A way to overcome this would be to use other verbs and encourage pupils to interchange these throughout their essays. Some ideas are shared below.

It is essential to value the text as a construct, written by the author. This will allow pupils to consider the big ideas and concepts of the text as a whole. A key way of achieving this is through the use of analytical and evaluative verbs (implies, reinforces, depicts, embodies). By including the author's surname and then hedging with an adverb, a powerful sentence can be constructed.

Author's surname + adverb + analytical verb

For example:

Shakespeare cleverly controls Macbeth's rhetoric to demonstrate that even a murderer can be capable of poetic verse.

This can be extended by exploring alternative meanings, demonstrating a perceptive and critical interpretation.

Author's surname + adverb + analytical verb + alternative meaning

For example:

Not only does Shakespeare subtly explore Macbeth's constant need to perform a role in society, but he also enforces the recurring motif of clothing to demonstrate that Macbeth's role is predestined.

This method is known as the '4 As' and has been influenced by *The Writing Revolution* (Hochman, 2012). Chris Curtis also writes about constructing powerful sentences for academic writing in his book *How to Teach English* (2019). He lists a number of strategies to micro-teach. For example, using adverbs at the start of sentences, using 'yet' or 'but' when explaining complex ideas, and developing interpretations by building up meaning through using 'suggests', 'shows' and 'symbolises' in quick succession.

A further strategy to value the character as a construct, which will enable pupils to discuss authorial intent, comes from the powerhouse Stuart Pryke, who often includes a statement and then a list of verbs for pupils to consider the author's intentions (see Pryke and Staniforth, 2020). The statement could be: 'Perhaps Shakespeare highlights Iago's malignant malevolence…' and the list of verbs could be: 'to criticise, to teach, to warn, to reveal the importance of and to challenge'. A further extension is to reference the author's surname and apply an action or emotion that they may have attached to their work. For example:

Author's surname + action/emotion

For example:

> *Priestley felt frustrated towards…*
> *Dickens is uncovering the reality of…*
> *Shakespeare is subtly dehumanising… to demonstrate…*

A further literary critic technique is using tentative language such as 'perhaps', 'might', 'could', 'maybe' and 'possibly' to hedge and demonstrate a contemplative and sensitive appraisal of the text.

Elleanor Larson's method goes further and encourages pupils to place a subordinate clause before the subject that refers to the author or the context, introducing wider ideas and showing the examiner that pupils can make critical connections. Try statements such as 'appalled by', 'driven by a desire to', 'an ardent believer in' and 'having witnessed'.

Academic essay-writing

The purpose of an academic essay is to carefully examine and evaluate a work of literature or an aspect of a work of literature.

Examining the different elements or methods used to convey meaning in a piece of literature is not an end in itself but rather a process to help pupils appreciate and understand the work of literature as a whole and what 'big conversation' the writer wanted to have about life, society and the human condition. Writing is the sharpened, focused expression of thoughts and study, but ultimately it boils down to the development of an argument.

Writing an introduction is a really important skill in presenting a clear argument and really focusing on the big concepts within the question. Jennifer Webb's strategy for a structured introduction is that of 'Discuss, define, refine' (*How to Teach English Literature*, 2019). Here she envisages an 'arrowhead pointing down the page to the rest of the essay', beginning with the broader concepts of the question, narrowing to an explicit focus and finalising the introduction with a specific line of argument. A further strategy is that of the thesis statement – a restricted, precisely worded declarative sentence that states the purpose of an essay. There are a number of options for how to begin a thesis statement, including:

Verb:

> **Considering** *the significance of poverty in* A Christmas Carol, *it is not difficult to value the sense of social reform that Dickens and many others wanted to instigate.*

Double adjective and noun:

> **The social and cultural portrayal of Edwardian women** *is so deeply intertwined in* An Inspector Calls *that the objectification of Sheila and Eva seems to be accepted by the matriarch, Mrs Birling.*

Adverb:

> **Clearly** *class injustice is vilified in* A Christmas Carol *through Dickens's grotesque depiction of Ignorance and Want.*

'Not only, but also':

> **Not only** *are the personal relationships within the novel key to exploring the wider social issues,* **but also** *they function as a means to connect the reader to concepts that seem condescending and patronising.*

'So, so':

> *Family is* **so** *significant to the reader's engagement with the Cratchits,* **so** *integral to our ultimate understanding of Victorian society, that even small acts of familial support and friendship could be deemed to be highly impactful.*

Contextual lead:

> **Victorian society was driven by the male patriarchy** *and as a result...*

Pupils need to be able to appreciate how a text is crafted to create meaning, and it's integral that they focus on their interpretation of meaning as much as possible. A method to accomplish this is asking the questions, 'What does this mean?' and 'What does this suggest?'. Pupils can then explore and analyse language by relating back to what, how and why. By questioning the quotation itself, pupils can then elaborate on their interpretation, valuing the different layers of meaning. Pupils should be encouraged to zoom in on particular words within the embedded quotation and discuss the alternative meanings, whilst applying a linguistic focus using word classes or devices. This should be modelled by teachers as it will also raise the misconception of feature-spotting, which is something we do not want to encourage.

Applying context can also be a challenge for pupils as they battle with the thin line between a history essay and a literary essay. But it is imperative to include as we need to make pupils aware that literature does not exist in a vacuum; the text is part of a wider conversation on the human condition in society. When including context in your writing, it can be as simple and as subtle as including Tier 2 vocabulary, such as poverty, workhouses and the Poor Law. It can also be the mention of the particular society in which the text was written, such as Victorian or Edwardian. Context does not need to be weighty; it must be a supportive element in a pupil's exploration of meaning. This is also a perfect opportunity for pupils to value the alternative meanings within the text. For example, pupils are aware that there are two readerships – the contemporary and the modern. Both of these exist at the same time of reading but through the consideration of context and authorship, pupils can feel confident to discuss these in greater detail.

The concluding paragraph of an academic essay might restate the original thesis statement but in different words. Pupils should summarise the main points that they have made or make a relevant comment about the literary work that they have analysed but from a different perspective. For example, the following is a concluding paragraph from an essay on Browning's poem 'My Last Duchess':

'If Browning's Duke has any redeeming qualities, they fail to appear in the poem. Ultimately, the reader's opinion of the Duke is not a favourable one, and it is clear that Browning uses him as a vehicle to criticise the objectification of women by men in powerful positions.'

Writing comparisons

Comparisons can be tricky for most pupils, especially when it comes to poetry. This is the most challenging type of literary discussion that pupils will undertake. Most, if not all, exam boards include poetry on their specifications and it is often the least answered element of the exam. But it is not something that pupils should shy away from, especially the unseen element. Encourage pupils to value an unseen poem using the 'Holy Triumvirate': title, first and last line. This will give pupils an overall perception of the poem before they tackle the analysis on their second or third reading. Pupils could also address the '4 Ms': mood, meaning, message and me (personal response) as a method of approach. Either way, pupils must establish an immediate connection with the unseen poem to develop a clear interpretation that will be explored in their essay.

Understanding the complexities and subtleties of a comparison question is how we, as teachers, can equip pupils to make meaningful connections between two texts. Ultimately, we want pupils to find common links between both texts as well as discussing what arises from their exploration of the texts' fundamental similarities and differences. A perceptive and assured comparative essay will notice that what may seem to be a sound similarity is actually a subtle difference, while still focusing on the wider picture. With this in mind, the best approach is a blended approach – one where a pupil can seamlessly transition from similarities to differences, including judicious evidence:

Introduction
Paragraph One – Text A and B
Paragraph Two – Text A and B
Paragraph Three – Text A and B
Conclusion

This particular essay structure will encourage pupils to discuss both texts together – it is the most effective and efficient method of comparing.

Pupils should start a paragraph with a topic sentence that discusses a similarity across both texts. For example, 'Both "Ozymandias" and "London" subtly criticise corrupt governments' would be an immediate similarity but, as teachers, we are aware that the poets have constructed this perception through varying methods. This would then form the pupils' comment on the different methods that these poets employed to achieve this overall reading. For example, 'Shelley comments on the disintegration of absolute power as it cannot stand the test of time, while Blake accuses the powerful Victorian institutions of not supporting those less fortunate.' The construction of these comparative sentences looks like this:

Both + author's name/text name + and + author's name/ text name + adverb + verb + point of similarity

Author's name/text name + verb + point of difference + comparative + author's name/text name + verb + point of difference

An essential process for constructing a comparison response is planning. This can be done whilst pupils annotate their prescribed text and it can be simply labelling the annotations 1 to 3 or it could be something more substantial, for example, the points of comparison; contextual connections; methods used by the author; or subtle references to the theme provided by the question. Sometimes pupils panic if, on the third reading of a poem, a new idea emerges that counteracts what they have already stated, but we must encourage their exploration. Neil Bowen and Michael Meally state that a 'good essay [is] exploratory [as] writing is a form of thinking and thinking is always dynamic and in flux' (*The Art of Writing English Literature Essays*, 2015).

That said, it also comes down to time management and reflecting back on what pupils have written. For example, if pupils are starting to notice that their line of argument is fluctuating, encourage them to edit their introduction or account for their tangent in the conclusion. This will ultimately demonstrate a critical perspective as well as an alternative interpretation.

Powerful openings: strategies to avoid 'I am writing to'

Success in AO5 (content and organisation) and AO6 (spelling, sentence structure and vocabulary) of the GCSE specifications really means two things: is the writing engaging, interesting and thought-provoking? Is it written clearly, adhering to Standard English rules of grammar, spelling, and punctuation? Often, we find the latter easier than the former, as it is intransitive: spelling is either right or wrong. The former is more difficult to master, as it requires a deep and flexible knowledge of how to select and manipulate big ideas.

Exam boards have reported that the best answers in non-fiction have a clear sense of 'engagement with "big ideas" [and are] able to enhance and enrich their responses' (AQA, 2019). This is the nub of how to enable pupils to structure their openings in non-fiction. Explicitly teaching pupils how to structure a conceptualised response helps them to clarify their ideas at the start of their writing, before expanding upon those ideas in later paragraphs.

In *The Writing Revolution* (2017), Judith Hochman and Natalie Wexler state, 'Sentences are the building blocks of all writing.' Yet we've all been there ourselves when writing a letter or an email: 'Dear so and so, I am writing to…'. When we read this 25 plus times from pupils, it feels stale and, more importantly, misses a golden opportunity to show off strong knowledge of sentence structure, vocabulary, punctuation and style. So, how best to avoid this?

1. 'Imagine a world...'

Here is an example based on a question of banning the sale of cigarettes:

> *Imagine a world free from the poison of passive smoking; where half a million lives are saved; where bad breath and yellow teeth are eradicated: this can be possible if we take action now and ban the sale of cigarettes.*

This is a powerful 'opening sentence' to teach – because it provides such a cohesive overview for pupils to 'set out their stall'. In starting with the imperative 'imagine', pupils are immediately engaging their reader with the topic at hand. The sentence allows for the three main points of the argument, which will be expanded upon, to be encapsulated, as well as providing a clear viewpoint as expressed through the 'solution' after the colon. The inclusion of three clauses separated by semicolons implies a conceptualised response, and the final section can be manipulated as a statement or posed as a rhetorical question. This sentence can also 'bookend' a response, providing a circular narrative which allows pupils to demonstrate a sustained engagement with the perspective they are trying to communicate.

2. Appositives

An appositive is a noun or a noun phrase which provides more information about the noun. They add unnecessary but interesting detail; they are, in this way, a powerful tool to help pupils introduce their perspective on a given topic. For example:

Smoking, a disgusting habit that blights our societies, is a constant threat to public health.

A constant threat to public health, the poisonous fumes from cigarettes are a symbol of the destructive tendency of the society in which we live.

Explicitly teaching appositives as a way to avoid 'I am writing to' ensures that the pupil is concentrating on communicating their perspective and signposting the direction their argument will take.

3. 'The news this week has been dominated by...'

A handy introduction, which can remove the intimidation of 'how to start' without resorting to 'I am writing to…', is to teach pupils to start with this sentence stem immediately after the salutation or title of their piece.

The news this week has been dominated by reports of needless illnesses and deaths linked to passive smoking. This is a shocking state of affairs, yet the answer is simple…

The sentence stem implies a familiarity with the issue at stake, which in itself instils pupils with confidence. It harks back to the Aristotelian Triad component of ethos: the idea that the reader must believe that the writer is trustworthy and knowledgeable (see page 119 for more on this). Pupils can then follow this with their opinion, which, of course, they will present as fact.

How to write an effective non-fiction paragraph (T.M.C.)

In order for pupils to be effective writers, they must be able to sequence their thoughts and ideas. This, as mentioned in the research section above, does not always come easily for unconfident writers. This teaching method allows them to do just that. The idea was created by Claire Thompson, an assistant headteacher in London. T.M.C. stands for **T**opic sentence, **M**ain ideas and **C**oncluding sentence. It is a shorthand method that helps pupils to construct a well-planned and formulated paragraph and it fits for any type of transactional writing.

The method is introduced to pupils in the following format:

Topic sentence: a sentence that introduces the main idea of the paragraph.

Main ideas: a series of sentences that all develop, explain or describe ideas that link to the main idea.

Concluding sentence: a powerful sentence that summarises the main ideas explored.

Here is a model of T.M.C. in practice in a Year 9 English lesson:

Example of T.M.C. in practice

Unit: transactional writing
Topic: gender inequality
Paragraph topic: toxic masculinity
Topic sentence: Toxic masculinity is an example of the inequality that is a constant burden plaguing men.
Main ideas: Have you ever seen a man holding tears back, pretending he's not hurt or simply laughing off any insults thrown his way? I know I have. When you expect a male to ignore any emotional pain, you are causing damage. Damage that is not only impactful on males but on females too. Some believe that if society demands that men are brave, powerful and daring, women must be the opposite. This is not the case! It is not the case that men should not cry, nor that women should not be strong. It is not the case that men do not feel pain at the taunts they receive, nor that women are inferior. In 2019, suicide amongst males aged 20–45 was the

> greatest killer in the UK. Why? Because we expect our men and boys to 'man up' and suppress any emotional twang in them. This inequality is taking lives! When you shame someone into feeling a natural emotion, you are condemning them to depression, despair and total isolation.
> **Concluding sentence:** Our men deserve better!

It is imperative with this method that direct instruction is used to support pupils with their crafting and to prevent them from going off topic. Expert teacher guidance is key. To get to this stage, pupils must also have mastered topic sentences. Once they have understood the constituent parts, this method is a versatile tool for any transactional writing. The 'I do, we do, you do' modelling approach works best with this method, as well as some of the sentence crafting ideas already mentioned. The results of such an approach are incredibly well-crafted paragraphs that are a joy to read.

Rhetoric: constructing an argument

Rhetoric or effective argument has been around since the beginnings of civilisation itself. Once pupils understand its power, they are able to craft emotionally persuasive, convincing pieces of work. Roman orator Cicero believed that an effective argument consisted of five elements:

1. **Inventio:** the presentation of convincing arguments.

2. **Dipsitio:** effective organisation.

3. **Elocutio:** style and eloquence.

4. **Memoria:** memorable content.

5. **Pronuncio:** effective delivery.

By explaining these tenets to our pupils, they are given a depth of understanding about rhetoric that they can then apply to any style of rhetoric writing they choose to craft. These tenets are understood best when explored using models and examples of famous speeches that fit with the concept you have planned to teach your pupils.

Aristotle, a well-known Greek philosopher, often considered the father of rhetoric, also made a vital contribution to the art of rhetoric. He gave us ethos, logos and pathos.

Ethos: an appeal to morality.

Logos: an appeal to reason.

Pathos: an appeal to emotions.

These tenets are now considered to be the foundation of the art of rhetoric and it is imperative that pupils understand this declarative knowledge before they begin any writing tasks on rhetoric. Again, this knowledge is best taught alongside incredible rhetoric creations of our time. This topic is perfect for exploring great contemporary speakers and equally, it fits so well with the literature texts that we study, but without the foundations of rhetoric explicitly taught, pupils are left ill-prepared for this topic.

Once pupils have mastered the foundations of rhetoric, it is time to teach them how to put this into practice. Constructing a well-planned and formulated argument takes time and thoughtful consideration. One way in which pupils can plan and construct their argument is described below.

Create a thesis: This is the idea, theory or argument pupils want to prove.

Proof: Convincing evidence to support the thesis; the reasons that justify the argument. This could include empirical data, appeal to authority and even anecdotal evidence that supports the thesis. These ideas formulate the main body of their writing.

Counterarguments: These are ideas that support the opposite of what the thesis is trying to prove. By including them in their argument, pupils are able to show that they have considered both sides. This adds credibility to what they are saying.

Conclusion: A powerful and convincing summary of your main ideas. This should be linked back to the original thesis statement for maximum impact.

There is a lot to unpack here and, like all great teaching, it is best delivered in sequential chunks and constituent parts using some of the aforementioned ideas. Once mastered, however, pupils have an in-depth understanding of rhetoric, which offers them the ability to create powerful pieces of writing to express their views.

Narrative writing: where to begin?

There really is no definitive answer to this question. There are many factors at play which subject leaders and classroom teachers must consider: how much narrative writing have pupils studied previously? How long is the unit? Is it a traditional block curriculum, or is it spiralled or interleaved? One thing is certain, though: teachers should start with assessment. Diving straight into a unit simply because it is pre-planned or resourced, without first assessing the narrative writing ability of pupils, is ill-advised and could result in misunderstanding pupils' needs. The assessment need not be high stakes and doesn't have to result in feedback; what it should do is inform the planning of lessons that follow.

A good route into teaching narrative writing is to cover the art of crafting stories. There are many examples online of writers' scribbled plans pre-writing – Sylvia Plath's notes for *The Bell Jar*, J. K. Rowling's for her Harry Potter series, and Joseph Heller's timeline for *Catch-22* are notable examples. Sharing visual examples of writers' carefully sequenced timelines or detailed plans for character and setting are a valuable preamble to pupils engaging in this activity themselves. It shows them that successful writing is meticulously planned and not simply the result of inherent talent as they might believe. In fact, at the start of the unit, there is a case for explicitly teaching how to plan and sequence a narrative, giving pupils the opportunity to plan in the style of Plath et al., without actually following through with writing. Modelling this process first is, of course, vital to them being able to experience their own successes in doing this.

Whether for planning or writing, pictures, poems, video clips or even dreams can be excellent sources of inspiration. Pupils are often fascinated by stories of writers who have dreamt up masterpieces in their sleep. Asking pupils to keep a dream diary over the course of a creative writing unit and then bringing it in for the final week of narrative writing is a fruitful task; it also helps keep cliché narratives at bay as most pupils don't actually dream about explosions, car crashes, haunted houses, or any of the other commonplace ideas which seem to dominate their narrative choices when pressed for time in the classroom. This task is also particularly useful for those tricky pupils who claim to have no imagination!

Sharing pieces of art can also be an excellent way of prompting thought too, and it exposes pupils to work that is rich in cultural capital. They're not just looking at the artwork; they're deconstructing and discussing it, becoming art critics, and exploring the different places in the mind where art can take a person. Before sharing artwork, sharing the title can also be a great stimulus – Freud's *Two Japanese Wrestlers by a Sink* or Van Gogh's *Café Terrace at Night* are good starting points. Art tells narratives in the same way stories do. It would be an oversight not to include this in a unit on narrative writing. Conversely, there is an argument for short stories influencing pupils' artwork in the art curriculum, but perhaps that is a matter for another book.

Descriptive writing: where to begin?

Much the same as the above, there are many factors to consider, but starting with a strong stimulus that prompts pupils' thinking is a good route into descriptive writing. As descriptive writing tends to have less action than narrative writing, it is useful to first use photographs which are rich in content and then strip them back to more simple images as the unit progresses and pupils' skills are built up.

The box method is a superb way of getting pupils to consider more minor details in their descriptions of settings. Give the pupils an image and ask them to draw five boxes on this image, choosing one box for each of the following:

- **Panoramic:** the largest box, and a general overview of the whole setting.

- **Pathetic fallacy:** some aspect of weather that they will use to establish the mood.

- **Personification:** something they will personify (nature is particularly effective here – share Daphne Du Maurier's opening to *Rebecca* to inspire pupils).

- **Zooming in on an insignificant detail:** getting pupils to choose something small and spend time crafting their description of it, such as a clock face or a rusty padlock.

- **Person or animal:** describing from a distance a living being in their setting.

This method can, of course, be adapted relatively simply for indoor settings or descriptions of character too.

When using the box method, it is important to guide pupils' practice, carefully showing them how to use this approach to craft a successful description. Planning your own alongside the pupils is key; it gives you the opportunity to explicitly show them how a writer makes meticulous plans pre-writing. Don't overlook modelling how to choose the boxes. It is important not to disregard this step – a poor box choice could yield poor results. Following this, deal with each box in turn and teach how to build up elements of description within that field. For example, for pathetic fallacy, you would want to look first at sensory language related to different kinds of weather and then consider how to choose appropriate verbs and adjectives to accompany it.

Because the planning process should be lengthy and well thought out, it is important to put aside a number of lessons to delve into each area in enough depth. You wouldn't expect a writer to produce a description per lesson, so don't expect it of your pupils, especially at Key Stage 3. Producing full pieces in the time limits of an exam is a skill best saved for GCSE.

Of course, this is just one method for first approaching description. There are many other options you might like to try. Mimicking great writers' characters and descriptions is one such profitable task. It gives pupils interesting grammatical structures to imitate, and potentially removes anxiety over their own accuracy, allowing them to focus on judicious language selections instead.

However you decide to first approach writing with pupils, remember this: good writing takes time and planning. Rushing the planning process and asking pupils to produce whole texts from the outset is a schoolchild error and perpetuates the mistaken idea that good writing somehow just falls out of good writers' pens.

Making the abstract concrete

One of the biggest hurdles that teachers face regularly in the classroom is the aversion to extended writing, be this creative, transactional or academic. Often, this is because of two reasons. Either because pupils don't have the requisite skill set to take on such a mammoth task independently, or they lack the intrinsic motivation to see it through. Tasks such as 'Write a description suggested by this image' or 'Write a speech where you argue that homework should be banned' may, on the surface, appear to give guidance and purpose, but they are, after all, abstract conceptualisations. These audiences and purposes are not real, but made up, and pupils can see right through them.

Our challenge is to make our learners see the point of this writing, to make these abstract ideas come alive through concrete avenues. Here are some ways we can achieve this.

Competitions

Use competitions to lure pupils in; develop their extrinsic motivation through the promise of prizes or the temptation to be published. There are plenty of external competitions to select from every month, ranging from short stories to essays and poetry. The BBC's short-story competition 500 Words, the Young Writers competitions and any topical competition organised by UNICEF are great places to start. Alternatively, organise an internal competition and get your budding writers writing!

Connect with real people

Think of ways that you can connect pupils with their primary audience. Perhaps they can write to their local MP to challenge them on their stance on a particular issue, or write to alumni persuading them to donate funds for the school library?

Find opportunities where the general public has been invited to express their points of view, for instance, consultation meetings organised by the local council regarding community development projects. Make pupils realise that their voice matters. If pupils are tasked with writing a speech, give them a stage, be this in a classroom, an assembly, a spoken word event, or in front of the school's SLT. Demystify the audience; bring them into the room.

Go for a walk

Writing descriptions or stories based on one-dimensional stimuli kills creativity even before the spark ignites. Take pupils out for a walk every season; the closer to nature, the better. Give them a scaffold for writing a description and then encourage adaptations to reflect the changing weather and atmosphere. What can they actually see, smell, hear, feel or even taste? Awaken their senses and let them experience the joy of playing with words to articulate various sensations. *The Winter Oak* by Yuri Nagibin is an excellent model for this activity.

School newsletter, blog or vlog

Whatever works, whatever motivates them, create these avenues. Give them a space for their writing to be published, to be read, to be celebrated. This could be a regular club or an annual booklet of great writing collated through classroom work or independently by pupils. Let pupils see the impact of the written word in action. Writing in its truest sense is not intended for an exam booklet, and our pupils need to be reminded of this on a regular basis. Make the abstract concrete with as many connections as possible.

Summary

- Remember that writing is a challenging skill for pupils and does not always come naturally to them. Start with word classes and sentence-building and go from there.
- If we want to change the statistics on pupils' writing, we must first overcome the cognitive constraints of writing. Contextualise writing tasks, use syntax and symbolism and chunk into small, manageable tasks.
- Modelling is key in supporting reluctant writers to get started. Use the 'I do, we do, you do' model.
- Offer real-world writing opportunities to avoid the abstract nature of writing tasks. For example, write to an MP and await a response!

6

Reading in English

*Mary Hind-Portley, Kaley Macis-Riley,
Lyndsay Bawden, Davina Canham
and Fe Brewer*

Introduction

Reading is a long-standing part of education as one of the 'three Rs' (reading, writing and arithmetic). It is also decried by some pupils as entirely unnecessary in our classrooms: 'Why do I need English? I can already read!' Of course, as all English teachers know, reading is far more than a skill that enables us to function in the world. It is a skill that enables us to navigate the world, yes, but it is also a way to learn about ourselves and others; a way to journey to other worlds and build a repertoire of human experience that enables us to navigate not only the functional aspects of life, but also the hurdles, successes and struggles.

In our classrooms, reading becomes the gateway to our world and the wider world, and for that reason it is imperative that we teach it with thought and consideration, with precision and care, with dedication and diligence. It is not enough that we simply read aloud the words on a page and hope that pupils infer and understand what we want them to. This chapter will prompt you to think and evaluate the place that reading holds in the English curriculum, and how we can make the most of it in our classrooms.

Research and theory

In the EEF's 2019b report, 'Improving literacy in secondary schools', one of the seven recommendations to improve literacy in all subject areas was: 'Develop pupils' ability to read complex academic texts'. In this, the activation of prior knowledge was seen as a pivotal part of teaching reading. With powerful knowledge, and the provision of the cultural literacy that comes with it, we can improve pupils' comprehension of complex texts, using the strategies explored in the above document. However, comprehension is built on effective inference; not the other way around. According to Anne Kispal at the NFER (2007), 'the ability to draw inferences predetermines reading skills: that is, poor inferencing causes poor comprehension and not vice versa'. Therefore, we must, as English teachers, have a robust understanding of what inference is because, as Kispal says, 'Inferencing skills are important for reading comprehension, and also more widely in the area of literary criticism and other approaches to studying texts. The National Curriculum lays much emphasis on the skills of inference, especially at Key Stages 2 and 3.' In this section, we will explore Kispal's research on inference in further detail.

Inference

Inference is at the heart of reading. But what is inference and do we focus enough attention on teaching how to infer in our curriculum-planning?

The 2007 literature review, 'Effective teaching of inference skills for reading' by Anne Kispal, gathers together a range of research about inference and provides us with a deeper understanding of what inference is and how we can approach planning and enacting explicit teaching of this fundamental part of the act of reading.

Firstly, we need to consider what inference is and ensure, through CPD and planning, that all teachers in a team have a consistent understanding of it to ensure that all pupils are taught effectively. The introduction to the Kispal's review defines inference as:

> *'The ability to make inferences is, in simple terms, the ability to use two or more pieces of information from a text in order to arrive at a third piece of information that is implicit'.*

The most illuminating finding of the review was that 'the ability to draw inferences predetermines reading skills: that is, poor inferencing causes poor comprehension and not vice versa.' How does this finding make us consider or reconsider our approaches to the active teaching of reading in our classrooms and departments? What makes effective teaching of inference?

Firstly, Kispal states that the research evidence reviewed identifies the following as being important for making inferences well:

- being an active reader who wants to make sense of the text

- monitoring comprehension and repairing misunderstandings

- having a rich vocabulary

- having a competent working memory.

Secondly, we need to be aware that effective inference needs wide background knowledge as well as sharing or being familiar with the cultural background of the text. The pupils in our classrooms may come from a wider range of cultural, religious and ethnic backgrounds or some schools may be largely monocultural. So, we need to develop our understanding of texts from a range of cultures to support pupils who may be familiar only with a narrow range of experience.

Therefore, we need to consider and then develop the most effective pedagogical approaches to support the development of the above. This includes:

- teacher modelling: making the active reading process explicit and concrete

- pre-teaching Tier 2 and Tier 3 vocabulary and modelling how to identify significant vocabulary choices and how they help readers to infer

- supporting pupils' understanding of 'showing, not telling' in the texts they read

- vocalising our thought processes during reading

- making explicit text structure and how writers make anaphoric and cataphoric references

- planning high-quality probing questions to ensure pupils' thinking and reading of the text are drawn out.

How do we support department members to do the above effectively?

- Use Kispal's literature review as pre-CPD reading (this is freely available online; see the references for the link).

- Set aside CPD time to explore and practise the above.

- Agree key points where explicit teaching of inference will take place (as well as ensuring that it will take place where needed as part of responsive teaching).

- Perhaps agree a common language across the department (note: you should ensure staff understand the difference between inference and implication).

- Perhaps have agreed strategies in workbooks or exercise books.

Putting it into practice

Approaching texts with a literary eye

When it comes to approaching a text, for too long, English teachers have fallen into the trap of reading chapter by chapter, analysing as they go. However, surely the very point of our subject is to read the text as it was intended, in its full form, and to understand its purpose as a construct. Can we ever truly analyse a text and its components prior to (literally) knowing the full story?

In this section, we explore how to approach a text in order to allow pupils to learn powerful knowledge, to decode meaning and to explore concepts presented.

What first?

With any text, be it nineteenth century, contemporary or a play script, teachers must plan to 'front-load' the contextual knowledge required to understand not only the content, but the idea of the text as a construct. If a pupil knows nothing of the social injustice in nineteenth-century London, can they ever truly understand *Oliver Twist* or *Jane Eyre*? If a pupil knows very little about the American economy in the 1920s to 1940s, can they ever really understand the depth that is explored in

The Great Gatsby or *Of Mice and Men*? How does a pupil's understanding of the Garden of Eden allow for a deeper understanding of *Macbeth*? All of these types of questions are what we must ask ourselves when looking at beginning to read a new text, with a class or cohort.

Suggest to your head of department that you sit down as a team, and establish what it is that pupils need to know about the social, historical and political context of the text, and explore the hinterland that pupils need in order to trigger curiosity and awe from a text. How can we take our pupils on a journey through a text? Which powerful knowledge will allow our pupils to decode a text and its components?

Cold reading and checking for understanding

Reading a text from start to finish is the best engagement tool to use with a class. Immerse pupils within the story, allow them to journey along with the characters, and you'll see no need for, as Daniel Willingham (2009) refers to them, 'attention grabbers'. The book is the hook, if you will. Any other attempt to get pupils' attention will, as Willingham explains, continue to 'get [the pupils'] attention – that is, to distract them, once the teacher was ready for them to think about something else'.

Don't stage a crime scene with props to introduce Priestley's *An Inspector Calls*, don't dress up in a toga and garland to introduce the origins of rhetoric. If you do, pupils will only remember what they thought about, and – in this case – that is the crime tape and bottle of bleach, or a teacher in a toga.

Teachers should read the text aloud to a class. Why? Because they are the 'best readers in the room, and this allows for pupils to hear the correct pronunciation of words' (Rowlands and Riley, 2021). We cannot simply assume that they know each word, and expect them to read it aloud and understand it. As Alex Quigley (2020) explains, 'without rich language experiences earlier on, we can predict that gaps will emerge in later reading' (Quigley, 2020). We teach pupils how to read like literary experts, by allowing them to hear literary experts reading.

In Chapter 7, we explore the importance of targeted vocabulary instruction, not just in our subject, but in all. Much of what is said later in that chapter can be linked to the concept of a cold read also. A cold read is only successful if vocabulary is taught explicitly.

As with any approach to a curriculum, a cold read is something that needs very careful consideration, and is something that is done differently in a number of different schools by different people. However a cold read is undertaken, one must plan to check for understanding throughout. It may well be that you chunk the text by chapters or sections and provide a formative check of understanding this way.

What does a cold read look like?

On the following page is an example of a cold read of *A Christmas Carol,* using questioning to check for understanding.

Example

Stage 1: Front-loading of contextual knowledge (mentioned prior).
Stage 2: Cold read

- Preface and stave one:
  ○ vocabulary
  ○ read
  ○ review.

| What is the first line of the novella? | Which adjective is used to describe Scrooge's voice? | Who is Scrooge's nephew? | What is the chain that Marley wears, as a ghost, symbolic of? | What do the charity men ask Scrooge for? |
| Finish the quotation: 'Darkness was _____ and Scrooge liked it.' | What is the name of Scrooge's clerk? | Describe the weather in this chapter, in no more than ten words. | How does the preface teach us about Dickens's intentions? | What does Marley say will visit Scrooge? |

- Stave two:
  - vocabulary
  - read
  - review (including questions used prior).

In your own words, describe the appearance of the Ghost of Christmas Past.	What is the name of Scrooge's sister?	What does Belle say has replaced her?	Give two examples of things or people that the ghost shows to Scrooge.
How are we made to feel sorry for Scrooge in this stave?	Complete the quotation: 'Our contract is an ____ one.'	Scrooge tells the ghost that he is torturing him. What does this mean?	What does the Ghost of Christmas Past hold?

- Stave three:
  - vocabulary
  - read
  - review (including questions used prior).

| Where does Scrooge find the Ghost of Christmas Present? | Who/What is the animal that Fred is thinking of in the game of 'Yes or No' that the spirit shows to Scrooge? | What are the names of the two children that appear from beneath the ghost's robe? | Complete the quotation: 'Come in and _____ me, man.' |
| Which words does the spirit repeat back to Scrooge to make him feel ashamed? | Why does the ghost wear an empty scabbard? | What is the name of the Cratchit's sick child? | Mrs Cratchit wears a 'twice-turned gown'. What does this suggest? |

- Stave four:
  - ○ vocabulary
  - ○ read
  - ○ review (including questions used prior).

Why do the young couple rejoice at hearing of Scrooge's death?	Complete the quotation: 'Let me see some _____ connected with a death.'	Whose death does the spirit take Scrooge to see?	Which of Scrooge's belongings does the charwoman attempt to sell to Old Joe?
In your own words, describe the Ghost of Christmas Yet to Come.	Finish the quotation: 'The Phantom slowly, _____ _____ approached.'	Why has Bob Cratchit 'been walking a little slower the past few evenings'?	When Bob breaks down following the death of Tiny Tim, he describes him as 'my _____ little _____'.

- Stave five:
  - vocabulary
  - read
  - review (including questions used prior).

| Finish the quotation: 'I am as _____ as a feather.' | In your own words, compare Scrooge at the start of the book to Scrooge in this stave. | How much money does Scrooge offer the boy if he returns with a turkey in five minutes? | Where does Scrooge plan to send the turkey he purchases? |
| What joke does Scrooge play on Bob? | When Scrooge tells Bob that he will 'raise [his] salary', how does Bob react? | What did Scrooge become to Tiny Tim? | Complete the quotation, from the final line of the novella: 'God bless us, _____.' |

By reading the texts in this structured way, you allow for reflective teaching. Explore vocabulary, read aloud, check for understanding, address misconceptions, re-teach and move forward.

Approaching drama texts

Let's be honest, most of us have a near-traumatic memory of someone reading *Romeo and Juliet* at a snail's pace with all the enthusiasm of a wet dishcloth, robbing the text of all its meaning. The truth is, reading plays is hard (especially Shakespeare plays) and it's different to reading prose. Also, the rules of reality are different with plays: people stay on stage, clearly within the hearing range of others, and yet they are unheard; actors wander around unseen; bundles of blankets are cradled as babies. Unlike other forms, plays require a suspension of disbelief that, unless one is familiar with the 'rules' of theatre, simply doesn't make any sense. As such, we need to consider some specific elements when reading play texts with our classes.

Capturing 'from page to stage'

No matter how brilliant your pupils are, they are unlikely to match the eloquence and potency of a professional, particularly at key moments of a play: they are unlikely to convey the extent of Mr Birling's fear and panic in Act 3 of *An Inspector Calls* or the contrasting displays of Lady Macbeth's ruthless ambition and disturbed paranoia. For these moments, there's really no substitute for a good performance such as those available from the National Theatre or the Royal Shakespeare Company. It is important for pupils to watch a play as it was intended to be conveyed: in its theatrical context. However, choosing an adaptation that is as true to the text as possible is incredibly important. Yes, we all love Baz Luhrmann's interpretation of Mercutio, but is it the right one to show as we introduce the play to novices? Absolutely, categorically not. No English teacher wants to read an essay on the presentation of conflict in *Romeo and Juliet* which is full of references to the petrol station, car chases, a helicopter and guns.

It is important to use a stage production that is professional and true to the original. Yes, directors and producers will adapt a play and have every right to use their artistic licence, but watching these performances can come after a 'cold view' of a drama text.

The visceral multi-sensory experience of a film production can substantially influence pupils' impressions of play texts (we've all experienced the 'Benvolio, the one with ginger hair' phenomenon) and it's important that we use film productions to consolidate understanding, rather than allowing them to be the understanding. However, there are a number of National Theatre, Digital Theatre+ and Globe performances that are incredibly close to how dramatic texts would have been intended to be staged by their writers. Draw on these because once a pupil sees a play performed, it comes to life and they understand it. After all, most English teachers have Shakespeare's works on a bookshelf somewhere, but few of those have ever read said works front to back; the printed texts are often used for reference purposes, post-viewing.

Reading drama in the English classroom

This is a contentious topic. Many advocate for pupils needing to read the lines of a play in order to understand them; others think that this practice is, in itself, why so many people are strongly opposed to such an idea. The camp in which you sit depends entirely on the context of your school and cohort: time given to English lessons, the demographic and cultural literacy of your pupils, the prior exposure to theatre, and so on.

However, I think we can all draw on conversations with other adults (usually not English teachers) about how 'boring' they found Shakespeare at school and how they 'didn't see the point then, and still don't'. This is, most likely, down to the dry reading of plays in a classroom setting, whereby pupils were made to read language that they didn't understand, pronounce words that dumbfounded them, and where what was intended to be a performance of splendour was – instead – a monotonous reading that made little sense to them.

It's important to note here that English departments could also work alongside the drama departments for some mutually beneficial cross-curricular planning in which pupils explore important extracts or theatrical methods, with performance and physical exploration of the text being in the drama classroom, whilst comprehension and analysis takes place in the English classroom.

Rhythm and rhyme

Verse, blank verse and prose carry meaning in a way that our pupils don't come across in other forms. Plays look like books, but they aren't, so pupils don't always notice subtle changes between verse and prose. Offering pupils extracts from different sections of the same play can make these distinctions more concrete, particularly when they're accompanied by discussions around the social class or emotional state of the characters. Once you've established that Othello usually speaks in blank verse, you can discuss why Shakespeare changes his speech to prose later, and what additional meaning that would carry.

Approaching pre-1914 texts

Reading is reading, but when we add in a different time or world with different perspectives, social structures or societal norms, the meaning behind texts can be skewed. While pre-teaching key contextual details is invaluable, pupils may still struggle with the conceptual and contextual demands of texts written in times so different from their own. Here are some specific challenges that you may need to help students overcome.

Archaic language

Invariably there will be language in pre-1914 texts that pupils will be unfamiliar with. Moreover, there will inevitably be an array of words that pupils – quite frankly – simply don't need to know. While we could spend hours explaining the eccentric and plentiful references made by Dickens, it's more important that we prioritise the pre-teaching of high leverage words and explore the purpose of those references. For example, what exactly all of those foods are that Dickens describes in Stave 3 of *A Christmas Carol* is unimportant, but their existence within the text is: that's our focus because that's where meaning is conveyed.

The 'but it's obvious' thing

One of life's key threshold concepts is hindsight, and this applies to literature as well. Yes, to us it is obvious that killing a king is never a good idea; it's obvious that beasts and witches aren't real; it's obvious that you can't stitch together bits of a corpse and bring it to life. This, like when reading plays, is a time when we almost have to ask pupils to suspend their disbelief and simply accept that people believed different things and that things, well, weren't as 'obvious' as they are now. Contemporary non-fiction can help here: the British Newspaper Archive, the British Library and CommonLit can be a great source of texts to support this.

Origins, production and printing

We often overlook the material history of older texts. Given the ease and availability of books these days, we neglect to acknowledge the privilege of this and how modern it is. Acknowledging that a text was first conceived and carried entirely orally, published as a serial, or edited heavily by someone other than the original writer (sometimes posthumously, as with Mary Shelley's very successful editing of Percy Shelley's poetry) can add an additional layer of understanding we wouldn't otherwise address. This is particularly important with early-modern literature and pre-nineteenth-century plays (as addressed in Chapter 4).

Adapting approaches for struggling readers

For a range of reasons, almost 148,000 11-year-olds enter our secondary schools every year unable to read 'well' (Read On, Get On, 2015). For children from low-income families, this figure rises to almost two in five. While this picture varies dramatically across the country, it is fair to say that most of us will encounter pupils who struggle to read for a number of reasons.

When considering this, there is a clear and important distinction to be made between those who are struggling to read and those who are reluctant to read. While the latter may not wish to read or engage well with reading, they're unlikely to struggle too much in life. For the former, the picture may be very different. While the foundations for successful reading are laid long before pupils reach secondary school, that doesn't mean that we can bow out and accept that struggling readers will forever be struggling readers; if we don't challenge this, then who will?

Model good reading behaviours

Many of us have visualisers in our classrooms now and we can use them to support our readers. Often, pupils who would benefit from tracking words with their finger or a ruler stop doing so because their peers don't, so they perceive it as being a big red flag that they're struggling. If we model reading under a visualiser using our finger or a ruler, we make it a norm. Pupils who may not wish to follow along in their book might follow our finger on the board instead. A simple change makes things just a little easier for our struggling readers.

Summarise first

Before beginning a chapter or extract, give pupils a brief overview of what to expect. While it may feel as though you're 'spoiling' the experience, what you're actually doing is giving pupils a structure of signposts and moments to 'look for' so that they can navigate their way through passages step by step rather than trying to decode language and comprehend meaning while also trying to track a narrative.

Pre-discuss difficult words

Before reading a passage, ask pupils to be open with you and identify words that they're unsure about (sometimes this might even be that you identify the words they do know). Make a point of discussing these: their synonyms; examples of them being used in context; or places pupils may have heard them before. By pre-exploring the vocabulary, you remove one of the hurdles your struggling readers have to negotiate, enabling them to better engage with the meaning of the text.

If in doubt, re-read

For shorter extracts, give pupils a chance to engage multiple times (you may wish to combine this with the previous strategies) to allow them to decode, comprehend and understand over repeated exposure. This will also take the pressure off that 'first read' and allow pupils to become more familiar with vocabulary and meaning. You may also ask pupils to practise reading an extract to each other before reading an extract as a class in order to improve their fluency.

Reading for pleasure

Most English teachers read for pleasure, so it's sometimes easy for us to underestimate the struggle some pupils have in finding or accessing a book to read for fun. The sad truth is that more than 50 per cent of pupils read for pleasure for less than 15 minutes a day – and with the distractions of phones, television, the internet, social media, and growing poverty in the UK, this is a problem that is likely to increase.

One of the difficulties of reading for pleasure is finding suitable books; libraries have been shut across the UK and school funding has been tightened, meaning it is harder to provide appropriate books for pupils. To add to that, pupils' reading ages are frequently a barrier to reading enjoyment – remember the Read On, Get On statistics about how many pupils start secondary school unable to read well (see page 143). There is also a gender discrepancy; more girls than boys report that they enjoy reading, and that they read daily outside of school. This means that pupils are less likely to be able to access books with content that will interest them at a level they can comprehend unaided.

Reading for pleasure has been repeatedly found to have a correlation with academic success, and as educators we appreciate the value of those educational milestones: the good passes at GCSE, the offer of a university place, the acceptance onto an apprenticeship. But for English teachers, reading means more: it's a journey into strange and familiar worlds, seeing ourselves reflected in words in another time and place, knowledge about different cultures and their similarities with our own. It's about the human condition, and all that unites us. A love of stories, and sharing, and words, and beauty. Without reading for pleasure, these joys are denied to our pupils.

Because of the challenges of literacy, the allure of technology, finite school time, and book availability, it is more important than ever that schools create positive cultures around reading for pleasure. That means prioritising time for it in the school day; buying books (the right books!) for the library; employing a librarian; talking about books; running book clubs; communicating with adults at home about reading; having reading mentors; paired reading; guided reading… All of these – not one or two in isolation – enable schools to have a visible, evolving and vibrant reading culture. And that means pupils are much more likely to read for pleasure themselves, and unlock the wonder and joy reading independently brings.

When you're thinking about reading for pleasure, be aware that some books that young people may gravitate towards explore farts, spots, 'fit' boys and snot in those all-to-familiar, less challenging (and often heavily illustrated) books which dominate bookshelves in supermarkets. Rather than annihilate these, we need to consider what we want children's literature to be for our pupils. Do we want reading for pleasure to be about comfort reads or do we push pupils towards classic reads or those tackling challenging concepts?

Comfort reads

These might well be the reads about boy bands or snot. There are many bestselling writers out there whose books echo the existing lives and teenage dramas of our pupils. These might not challenge pupils' views or knowledge, but they offer entertainment. It is worth considering, however, how much exposure our pupils have to these; what is the purpose of education, after all, if it doesn't challenge what children already know?

Classic reads

We live in a world where what's considered 'classic' is being challenged, but the canon will likely remain the canon and it will continue to be alluded and referred to in popular culture. Encouraging our pupils to engage with canonical reads offers them an in-road to those allusions, enabling them to partake in wider culture.

Challenging concepts

There is an increasing market (although arguably this has existed for some time), for children's literature that challenges young people's thinking and offers them insight into concepts and cultures outside of their daily lives. Given the knowledge and empathy that can be gained through reading, these books are an important part of our pupils' reading 'diets' and can offer pupils a glimpse of worlds beyond their own which challenge their thinking. If we consider a primary function of children's literature to be socialisation and didacticism, reading books that introduce young people to the complexities of the modern world chimes with the very purpose of the genre, as it invites them into lessons that lay important blueprints for life.

In the classroom: teacher reading versus pupil reading

Beyond the traditional thinking of 'teacher reads to pupils' or 'pupils read aloud to other pupils', we can approach reading in a range of ways to focus on different elements that work together to form effective, enjoyable reading. We will explore some of these strategies below.

Reciprocal reading

Reciprocal reading is a cross-subject strategy for approaching reading an academic text. It harnesses metacognitive techniques to break down and make explicit the habits of expert readers into a series of steps designed to improve pupils' procedural knowledge of reading as well as their confidence and comprehension of texts.

The EEF (2019b) recommends the following steps to support pupils' comprehension of subject-specific material.

Activating prior knowledge
Pupils think about what they already know about a topic from reading or other experiences, such as visits to museums, and try to make meaningful links. This helps pupils to infer and elaborate, to fill in missing information and to build a fuller 'mental model' of the text.

Example: Pupils are asked to recall the 'push and pull factors' that determine international migration.

Prediction
Pupils predict what might happen as a text is read. This causes them to pay close attention to the text, which means they can closely monitor their own comprehension.

Example: Pupils could be asked to predict the impact of international migration on English seaside towns.

Questioning

Pupils generate their own questions about a text to check their comprehension and monitor their subject knowledge.

Example: Pupils generate five key questions on 'the impact of increased net migration into the UK since 2004'.

Clarifying

Pupils identify areas of uncertainty, which may be individual words or phrases, and seek information to clarify meaning.

Example: Pupils check they understand a graphic illustrating net migration figures presented alongside the text.

Summarising

Pupils summarise the meaning of sections of the text to consolidate and elaborate upon their understanding. This causes pupils to focus on the key content, which in turn supports comprehension monitoring. This can be supported using graphic organisers that illustrate concepts and the relationships between them.

Example: Pupils generate a short summary of the impact of internal migration on the UK since 2004.

*

Using this approach across the whole school, with tweaks for differing departments, can bring a consistency and effectiveness to the explicit teaching of reading to the benefit of all pupils, even those most confident, and will also support teachers, giving them a clear framework for scaffolding academic texts.

Reading ages

For teachers to be really clear in our understanding of our pupils' reading abilities, and to therefore know when we need to model, scaffold, and break down reading activities, all teachers must be aware of their pupils' reading data. Many of us will have seen pupils struggling to read in class when asked – one of the authors of this book has seen a Year 9 boy in tears because he couldn't read aloud the passage he was being asked to, and afterwards it came to light that his reading age was only nine years, and his teacher didn't know. How many young people will have been affected by such experiences?

The most straightforward way to ensure that reading ages are considered by teachers is to have the reading ages for every pupil on the school's management information system, alongside other data such as SATs and CATs. But reading ages change so ideally, testing for them should be undertaken twice yearly, as a minimum.

There are many reading-age tests on the market, and it's worth considering which will offer the best value for your context: which are taken and marked online; which are paper-based; which provide a report; which details and data are in the report; and whether you are paying for one test or unlimited tests in a fixed period. All these questions will need to be considered before you make this significant financial commitment.

Another benefit of testing for reading ages is that most testing is now accepted by the Joint Council for Qualifications (JQC) as evidence for special considerations in exams and coursework. As well as this, the testing will support you in identifying pupils who need further intervention in their reading, and the type of intervention required: phonics, fluency, inference, comprehension, and so on.

Without baselining pupils' reading abilities, there is also no way to be sure that pupils are progressing and keeping up chronologically with their reading age improvement. As an estimated 20 per cent of pupils start secondary school unable to read fluently, we have a moral duty to assess and intervene to improve this, which in turn will improve not only pupils' educational outcomes, but also their quality of life.

Exam questions

Exam success means helping students to know what the question is asking them to do. Therefore, questions need to be broken down with students to ensure they have the best chance of success. This is especially pertinent as the reading age for exam papers can sit above some of our students' reading ages. Many exam boards publish lists of command words and it is a good idea to share these with students so they have a point of reference. To support our students in becoming articulate communicators and critical thinkers is to give them a powerful gift. It helps them to navigate a world where words create all kinds of narratives.

Some common question styles include:

- a theme or character question (in English literature exams)

- a question about language and its effects (in GCSE English language exams)

- a statement or view which must be debated (this is often seen in A level English literature).

Here are some strategies that may help students to understand and interpret exam questions to ensure success.

Pick apart the question with synonyms
First write the question in the middle of a page and highlight the key words or steer for clarity. Then put ideas discussed with the class around it. Take a character question, for example:

How is Lady Macbeth presented to be a powerful woman?

Students will benefit from synonyms for the question steer 'powerful' – what do we mean by powerful in this context in

Macbeth? Synonyms for this could be 'manipulative', 'strong' and 'atypical', and this allows students to think of their own interpretations of the character rather than limiting them to one strand in their argument.

Consider the 'how'

Students need to be directed to consider what 'how' or 'the ways' mean when this appears in a question. Essentially, they need to understand it requires them to know which methods a writer uses to convey their character or theme. For grade 4 and above, students need to be able to show they understand the text is a crafted construct, with characters and not real people deliberately presented through certain methods for impact.

Consider the wider conversation the text is having with relation to the steer

Finally, students need to consider *why* the text does something and therefore what the big conversation is about the human condition or life that the writer wanted to have? Here we could ask students to consider what the text is doing: criticising, warning, exposing, challenging or highlighting, to help them see the wider picture. If we use the Lady Macbeth question, we might consider if *Macbeth* on a wider scale highlights the dangers of women who do not conform to society's dictum of subservient womanhood.

*

Once they have understood what the question is asking them to do, students need to pick arguments first before quotations. This is the best way. Students tend to pick quotations first, but this does not help them to create and thread a line of argument through their essay. Often we end up with stand alone paragraphs analysing single quotations. Once students have decided on their arguments they can then select high-value moments and evidence to illustrate them.

This breaking-down and planning would all lead into the thesis statement. Essentially, in writing their literary analysis, a student's objective is to convince the examiner that they have supported the idea they are developing. A thesis statement involves a declarative sentence that states the purpose of their essay. Indeed, it is the crux of the argument students are trying to make: their 'argument in a nutshell'. Show students exam board exemplars and previous students' introductions to read, annotate and rank, and discuss strengths or improvements. Advocate no first-person 'I' or second-person 'you' and that it should capture a clear argument with reasons. Thesis statements should be conceptual and use the key words of the question. Students may benefit from defining themes in the question and how they link to their texts. A class could practise by writing thesis statements on texts in pairs if that helps. The word 'through' is really excellent in helping to phrase thesis statements, for example:

Through the characters of Myrtle and Gatsby, Fitzgerald criticises the hollowness of the American Dream.

We then move into completing our own introductions, getting feedback and making tweaks. It is utterly vital to make time to allow for students to have a sharply focused introduction 'setting out their stall', because it crystallises for them what they are arguing. Furthermore, the examiner will be clear what the student is arguing and by association – hopefully – have a favourable opinion of your student and their essay right from the opening.

Summary

- Reading is a vital skill that empowers our pupils and enables them to learn about the human condition.
- Inference is at the heart of reading and must be taught in our classrooms.
- Different types of reading will require different approaches. This must be planned carefully.

7

Vocabulary

*Lyndsay Bawden, Abigail Mann
and Fe Brewer*

Introduction

When Atwood wrote 'a word after a word after a word is power', she was right. She did, however, neglect to mention that it's not just any words, but the right words that hold the most power. David Crystal (2007) remarks that 'the big world has big words', and this lends itself beautifully to this chapter; there are so many young people who simply won't meet and learn to use those big words unless they are instructed, supported and inspired to do so.

Within the words we use every day lie both our history and our future. Every word in our language has a story, an evolution, and a rich plethora of meanings and connotations. The more familiar we are with the stories behind the words we use, the more we can navigate them, understanding their nuances and the layers of meaning they create, and moreover, the better we can weave them in for effect, conveying meaning with precision and beauty.

To complete Crystal's quotation: 'Education is the process of preparing us for the big world, and the big world has big words.' This chapter aims to discuss and develop how we, as English teachers, do just that.

Research and theory

The EEF's 2019b report 'Improving literacy in secondary schools' carefully analysed the existing research on literacy, including vocabulary acquisition, and came up with a list of seven key recommendations for the improvement of literacy in English secondary schools. The report finds that literacy is key to pupil success across the curriculum, and emphasises the imperative for all teachers to be teachers of literacy. Vocabulary knowledge is found to be one of the key indicators of academic success, and pupils from lower-income households are more likely to be familiar with fewer words than their more affluent peers. This tells us that as educators we have a moral imperative to work towards closing this disadvantage gap, and using research shows us the most effective ways of doing so.

Priority number two in the EEF report is: 'Provide targeted vocabulary instruction in every subject.' The report recommends the following key practices to support the teaching and learning of vocabulary:

- exploring common word roots

- undertaking 'word building' activities, such as matching prefixes and root words, for example

- encouraging independent word-learning strategies, such as how to break down words into parts and how to use dictionaries

- using graphic organisers and concept maps to break down complex academic terms in visual ways to aid understanding

- undertaking regular low-stakes assessment, such as quizzes, to provide multiple exposures to complex subject-specific vocabulary

- consistently signposting synonyms

- combining vocabulary development with spelling instruction.

This chapter will explore some of the practical ways teachers can utilise these findings in their classrooms and across the school, most of which are applicable to all subjects, not just English.

Putting it into practice

Developing a rich vocabulary

Imagine giving one of your pupils a straightforward task with – what you consider to be – a pretty pedestrian, straightforward opener. Then imagine they refuse to write anything, claiming, 'I can't write this, Miss. I don't sound like that!'

Imagine giving pupils this opening sentence: 'Good morning. My name is... and I'm here to talk to you about...' The pupil – and several others – simply could not identify with such lexis and syntax. They were not part of their language or their vocabulary, and as such they simply couldn't operate with them. While perhaps an extreme case, this is the reality for many of our pupils who come across words written by Dickens, Shakespeare or Shelley. They simply do not recognise them and, more importantly, cannot identify themselves as someone who ever would. Given the impact words can have on our identity, not simply as academic pupils but as people, we mustn't underestimate the impact that vocabulary-teaching can have on our pupils' academic development and also their personal development. But how do we introduce pupils to the world of 'big words'?

We can't introduce pupils to every big word; we don't have time and it isn't necessary. What we can do, though, is select powerful words that not only unlock meaning, but also nurture the confidence pupils need to 'crack open' the words we haven't had the chance to teach them.

Identify your 'big win' vocabulary

As our curriculum time is finite, we have to make decisions about what to do so that we have the chance to do those things well, and choosing vocabulary is no different. Mapping words across a curriculum is explored later in this chapter (see page 162), but it's worth noting early that when we choose our big wins well, our job becomes easier because we 'bump' into them more often and have more opportunities to utilise them.

For example, if the word 'masculine' is taught early in Key Stage 3, it can be revisited again and again throughout the curriculum: we can talk about different characters' contrasting masculine ideals in *Macbeth*, about ideas of masculinity and power in *An Inspector Calls*, and about toxic masculinity in society. We can use these words to 'trigger' discussion and retrieval practice. For example, if we're discussing the futility of Dr Jekyll's attempts to resist temptation, we can quickly revisit questions about other examples of futility: Ozymandias's attempt to hold eternal power; the soldier's attempts to drink away his post-traumatic stress disorder.

The more meanings we associate with words, the more we use them; the more we use them, the more they become part of our vocabulary, so giving pupils frequent exposure to big, powerful vocabulary – and opportunities to put this into practice – is of great importance.

Play with the building blocks

To quote Daniel Willingham (2009), 'the brain "privileges" stories'. By tapping into the etymology of words, we can facilitate curiosity and thinking about words, through exploring their stories and the patterns and relationships between them. Furthermore, when looking at common building blocks, we inevitably meet words pupils already know, utilising existing knowledge and extending it into the new.

For example, pupils know what 'press' means, but may not understand express, suppress or oppression. Here is an ideal opportunity to unpick those words, examining common Latin prefixes that build stories and relationships between words.

To take just one of these:

Press = push down + 'ex' = out

Therefore, express = out + press = a pushing out or release

If ex = out, then what other words can we unlock? Excite, explode, extend, extra-terrestrial, export, exclude, exhale.

All of a sudden, our adventure can take us on pathways that lead us onto words like city, applaud, tend, territory, port (a short step from transport, which has a rich and relevant path of its own), close, and plenty more. More importantly, we have a conversation about words pupils use every day, but will now see in a different light; as part of a rich tapestry of vocabulary they have at their fingertips.

Use the Frayer model

When we have more conceptual vocabulary to explore, completing Frayer models with pupils can be of great help. Exploration focuses on one word at a time and requires an exploration of definition, characteristics, examples and non-examples. As such, this is a very effective model for exploring

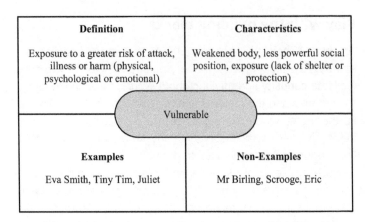

Definition	Characteristics
Exposure to a greater risk of attack, illness or harm (physical, psychological or emotional)	Weakened body, less powerful social position, exposure (lack of shelter or protection)

Vulnerable

Examples	Non-Examples
Eva Smith, Tiny Tim, Juliet	Mr Birling, Scrooge, Eric

FIGURE 7.1 *An example Frayer model for the word 'vulnerable'.*

literature where a plethora of characters and situations means pupils can utilise pre-existing knowledge when exploring a term, attaching new vocabulary to existing knowledge and making it more relevant and memorable.

Figure 7.1 shows an example Frayer model for the word 'vulnerable'.

Challenge colloquialisms

'How does Scrooge feel here?'
'He's gutted, Miss.'

A classic example of a pupil using their own vernacular to answer a question without thinking beyond the words they use every day. In a lesson, we could easily brush this off and take a different, perhaps more academic, answer from someone else, but we could also embrace moments like this as an opportunity to explore synonyms and how they work in different ways and different contexts. While we wouldn't say we're 'dismayed' at finding the corner shop had run out of our favourite chocolate, we would use it to describe Scrooge at points in *A Christmas Carol*. The context in which we use our vocabulary is as important as the vocabulary itself, so both need to be part of the discussion so that our pupils aren't only adding to their vocabulary, but are developing a greater understanding of the vocabulary they already possess.

Tiered vocabulary

For some years now, the terms Tier 2 and Tier 3 vocabulary have been littered about on teacher resources on social media, and for good reason. The terms originate from a brilliant book called *Bringing Words to Life* by Isobel Beck et al. (2013). Below is a breakdown of the three tiers of vocabulary which she talks about in her book.

- **Tier 1:** most basic words which typically appear in oral conversations, e.g. warm, cat, girl, swim. Learners are exposed to these words from a very young age, so readily become familiar with them and are likely to use them in their everyday language.
- **Tier 2:** words which are of high utility for mature language users and are found across a variety of domains, e.g. precede, auspicious, retrospect. As these words are characteristic of written text, and used more rarely in conversation, pupils are less likely to learn the words independently.
- **Tier 3:** words rarely used, which are limited to specific topics and domains, e.g. photosynthesis, machicolations. These words are probably best learnt when a specific need arises, like teaching subject-specific terminology in the context of a lesson.

It is a focus on Tier 2 words that is thought of as being the most productive approach to developing vocabulary-rich learners in the English classroom and beyond, with the aim of teaching around 400 new words per year.

Once clear on the different tiers of vocabulary, it is time to decide which Tier 2 words to use and why. Firstly, how important is the word chosen? Does it have a strong utility? Can it be conceptually understood and will it be well suited to instructional teaching? The simple questions below can help you when deciding which words to choose.

- How useful is it? Will pupils meet it often? Will they find it in other texts? Will they use it to describe their own experiences?

- How does it relate to other words they know? Will it add more dimension to a topic covered?

- What does the word contribute in the situation or text?

Once you have decided upon the Tier 2 vocabulary you intend to teach, it goes without saying that you will need to map it carefully across your curriculum plan and schemes of learning. These words become the spine of your vocabulary-teaching across each unit. They should not, however, prevent you from teaching more Tier 2 vocabulary as your lessons progress, rather, they provide a solid foundation from which to build.

Mapping vocabulary through long-term planning

Cognitive science has taught us much about how we learn and how we, as educators, can harness the best bets for teaching our pupils, and this is something we can use to inform our teaching of vocabulary. Research has shown that it can take as many as 17 exposures to new vocabulary for it to move into long-term memory and be easily accessed. For this reason, it's important that as well as explicitly teaching vocabulary, including its etymology and usages, we return to it, to retrieve it and strengthen pupils' recall of a word and its uses until they have been mastered. This holds true for every subject in school, not just English.

Mapping vocabulary through long-term planning allows us to utilise the curriculum to strengthen and develop pupils' vocabulary knowledge. There are various different ways to approach this, such as using already listed Tier 2 and 3 words, mapping them onto your curriculum, and signposting when they will be returned to for reinforcement and development. Another way is to use the curriculum itself to draw out the key vocabulary needed for the core, and underpinning concepts that run vertically and horizontally through the curriculum. For example, a repeated theme in your curriculum might be the representation of women; you might introduce the vocabulary 'femininity' in Year 7 through a literary character such as Nancy in *Oliver Twist*, and then repeat and develop the teaching and recalling of the word throughout their English study, culminating in a study of how Shakespeare presents femininity through Lady Macbeth:

Year 7	Nancy	Femininity: maternal instinct, sympathetic character, stereotypical, lack of power.
Year 8	Juliet	Femininity: breaks social conventions, challenges norms of behaviour, chaste and virtuous.
Year 9	Curley's wife	Femininity: sexuality as dangerous, women as corrupters, victim of male violence.
Year 10	Sheila	Femininity: change from ignorance to awareness, from passive to active.
Year 11	Lady Macbeth	Femininity: subversion of feminine traits of maternal instinct, power and influence, reversion to stereotypical mental weakness?

Here we can see the word femininity being used in a relatively simple and straightforward way in Year 7, and then being developed and used as a way of challenging representations of women through more complex explorations of characters and ideas as the curriculum progresses, thus building pupils' schema in relation to the word. If you also use the benefits of the testing effect and regularly quiz the pupils on the meanings and uses of the word, you are helping them to strengthen their understanding and recall of the vocabulary, so it is primed for them to use it again in a similar or different context.

It is only by deliberately mapping the key vocabulary of the curriculum that you can ensure vocabulary is purposefully recalled and developed. Hence you are allowing sufficient exposures to the words to ensure mastery by pupils, otherwise the building of vocabulary is left to chance, is random, and we therefore cannot be sure we have taught the pupils, or that they have really learnt, the most important words we need them to know.

Harnessing form time

Recent reforms in exam specifications and reports from regulatory bodies such as Ofsted have reinforced that literacy is the responsibility of all teachers, not just those teaching English. Disciplinary literacy, that is, specific approaches to the individual nuances of literacy in different subjects, is becoming recognised as key to pupils' success in different domains. However, an intersecting time in most schools, where the boundaries of curriculum are blurred, is form time. For many schools, this is 20 minutes a day, which can be spent on very important aspects of the school day, such as assemblies, PSHE, equipment checks, and so on. However, if we recognise the significant barrier to pupils' progress across the curriculum that is posed by poor literacy knowledge, then there is an opportunity here to use that time to make huge gains for all pupils; we make time for what we consider to be important.

There are various ways to use this time productively, a few suggestions being as follows.

Word of the week

Really this should be named 'root word of the week', but it's not as catchy! This is where the whole school focuses on a particular Greek or Latin etymology each week through form time, and embeds it in the school day via the curriculum. This is really powerful because 60 per cent of words in English have Latin or Greek roots. The most effective usages introduce the word(s) using call and response to practise the pronunciation, and the words are broken down into syllables. Each of the target words is then used in a sentence to model its contextual usage, and the words are used around the school in lessons and assemblies, and tied into the house or rewards system. An example is shown in Figure 7.2.

Silent reading or library time

Another way to harness the power of reading to improve vocabulary, comprehension and knowledge acquisition is through pupils' private reading. Research from Kirsch et al. found that engaged reading time is key to reading achievement (2002), and further research has shown that five to 14 minutes of reading per day was linked to sluggish gains in reading age, below the national average (Renaissance Learning, 2015), but that more than 15 minutes of reading led to accelerated gains. This is backed up by the findings from the National Center for Education Statistics, which showed that reading for 20 minutes

Anti: against, opposite (Greek word root)

- **Anti**septic preventing the growth of disease-causing microorganisms.

- **Anti**biotic a medicine (such as penicillin or its derivatives) that inhibits the growth of or destroys microorganisms.
- This video explains how antibiotics work:
  https://www.youtube.com/watch?v=X1GT2bKgci8

- **Anti**social not sociable or wanting the company of others.

Reminder
Use each
word in a
sentence

Week beginning 14th September

Anti: against, opposite

Word use questions
- What might antithesis be?
- What might an anti-climax be? (-ist)

Thinking questions – use the target words in your response
1. Would you rather be antisocial or gregarious? Why?
2. As a class, how many antihero characters in books or movies can you think of?
3. How do you feel when you have to take antibiotics? Explain using one of these words: **because, but, so.**

Super challenge: What does anti**body** mean?

FIGURE 7.2 *Word of the Week: Anti*

per day equated to a likely score better than 90 per cent of peers on standardised tests (2013). On their own, fewer than 20 per cent of pupils read for 15 minutes or more a day (and this figure is on a downwards trend), which means that schools must intervene to provide the time and resources for it to happen.

One of the most astonishing benefits of reading daily is the vocabulary it exposes pupils to: if a pupil reads for 20 minutes a day at school, they will be exposed to over 1,800,000 words a year, compared with a pupil who only reads for one minute a day, who will be exposed to just 8,000. This gives a clear and powerful message that schools cannot ignore: making time for reading at school is imperative.

The pitfalls of silent independent reading are that teachers can disengage from the process and use it as admin time, rather than modelling their own reading, or talking to pupils about the books they are reading. The other common problem is pupils who 'fake' read, and will stare out of the window for 20 minutes with a book open in front of them! This is why fast reading is becoming more popular.

Fast reading

One in four 15-year-olds has a reading age of 12 or below, meaning they are unable to independently access many reading for pleasure books, as well as curriculum texts and exam papers. In a recent relatively small-scale study, the impact of 'just reading' challenging novels aloud to pupils every day was shown to have a huge impact on pupils' reading comprehension and reading ages, and this was particularly effective for weaker readers: 'Simply reading challenging, complex novels aloud and at a fast pace in each lesson repositioned "poorer readers" as "good" readers, giving them a more engaged, uninterrupted reading experience over a sustained period.' In 12 weeks, pupils made 8.5 months' progress, but poorer readers made 16 months' progress. As well as improving reading ages and comprehension, being read to, and encountering brilliant books pupils wouldn't otherwise access, has an ethical and social benefit: discussions around books can be shared, stories can be appreciated and enjoyed, cultural knowledge is transmitted, and vocabulary is learnt in context.

Form time is the perfect opportunity for this shared narrative around books and words to take place. It requires an investment from SLT into books, and for staff to be on board with the importance and skill of reading aloud and the benefits of sharing stories; it also, crucially, signals to pupils, parents and visitors the importance placed on literacy in the culture of the school.

*

These form-time measures all serve to highlight the significance of words, vocabulary and reading to the culture of a school, signposting its importance, and showing its value to every teacher in every subject for every pupil in every year group, and setting the tone for the rest of the day's learning. Enabling a word-rich environment to be encouraged and celebrated ensures all pupils are supported in acquiring the knowledge of words they need to be effective communicators and members of society.

Explicit vocabulary instruction

In *Bringing Words to Life*, Beck et al. (2013) argue that robust vocabulary instruction which 'involves directly explaining the meanings of words along with thought-provoking, playful and interactive follow-up' is an effective way of teaching pupils to adopt new vocabulary. It is important that the new words are seen multiple times in a frequent manner using various different approaches. This ensures that the learning activities involve deep processing from the pupils. In order to do this, the SEEC model, as outlined in *Closing the Vocabulary Gap* by Alex Quigley (2018), could be used. The model is outlined on the following page.

Select
This step is all about choosing the right words to teach. Questions you might consider are as follows. What words are most important to understanding this topic? How often are pupils likely to see this word repeated? What words are unlikely to be part of a pupil's prior knowledge, and so on.
Explain
This step is about explaining the word in detail to the pupils. Say the word carefully. Break it down phonetically. Use choral feedback so that pupils understand the pronunciation. Have it written down so pupils can see it and hear it. Offer multiple examples of it in use. Check understanding by asking pupils for examples.
Explore
There are multiple ways in which the word can be explored from the etymology or using multiple-choice quizzes and looking at common word families, antonyms and synonyms. All of these approaches allow the understanding of the word and its usage to deepen for our learners. The more exploration that occurs, the greater the chance of the pupils retaining the word and using it more frequently in their writing.
Consolidate
The final step of the process is to consolidate learning. Return to the word frequently. This works well as part of retrieval practice in subsequent lessons. Of course, any taught vocabulary is likely to come up again as part of a well-planned curriculum, so further opportunity to consolidate is made secure.

*

By adopting the methods shared in this chapter, you will ensure that your pupils develop a rich and exciting vocabulary that they can use time and again to their advantage.

Summary

- Vocabulary has the power to open up the world for our pupils. Dedicate time every lesson to building vocabulary with your pupils.
- It is important to identify your 'big win' vocabulary as part of your curriculum-planning and pre-teaching of any content. Map these out at the start of the year for successful vocabulary-building.
- Vocabulary development is every teacher's responsibility. All teachers should teach vocabulary instruction within their lessons, regardless of the subject. Tutor time should be harnessed, for vocabulary development.
- Disciplinary literacy plays a role in vocabulary development. Ensure subjects across the school know how to teach students to read, write and communicate effectively in their subjects.

8

The science of learning

Zara Shah and Abigail Mann

Introduction

In the quest to become a research-informed practitioner, the most challenging aspect is knowing where to begin. As the appetite for the development of practice and the interest in cognitive science grows, so does the availability of resources, many of which are easily accessible through the click of a few buttons. Two great places to start researching are the EEF and the Chartered College of Teaching. But filtering through, establishing efficacy, organising ideas and then converting them into practical and sustainable processes in the English classroom can be a daunting task to take on as an individual. That is where we come in. In this quest to become a research-informed practitioner, the most challenging aspect is indeed knowing where to begin, so it would be logical to begin with the ending in mind, by asking the question that we all want answered: how do our pupils learn and what can we do to make them learn better?

Research and theory

In order to answer this, we need to first understand how memory works. Storing something in our 'memory' isn't as simple as dragging and dropping a folder. Instead, we have to relate new information to what we already know. Cognitive psychologist Robert Bjork (1994) describes this process as 'semantic in nature': 'we store information in terms of its meaning to us'. In his highly influential book on cognitive science, *Why Don't Students Like School?*, Daniel Willingham (2009) describes memory as the 'residue of thought'. This means that in order for us to learn or remember anything, we first need to think about the information we are handling, to engage with it, to contextualise it and to interrogate it. To ensure that pupils remember what we teach, we must activate their thinking, the same way we are going to activate your thinking now, with these questions:

- How can we make our pupils think about new material in the context of what they already know?

- How can we help them to connect the dots and make links between existing and new knowledge?

- What type of scaffolding do we need to put in place to make pupils build visual representations of their understanding and build what we call 'schema'?

In cognitive science, a schema is a pattern of thought or behaviour that organises categories of information and the relationships among them; it is at the core of cementing memory. It is ever-developing, created by building on prior knowledge and filling any gaps in the information that we hold. It is what sets an expert apart from a novice. Experts refer to the wealth of complex schema that they have built over time, which limits strain on their thinking capacities and makes mental processing more efficient. If we were to consider schema as a visual metaphor, we could think about building blocks, with each colour representing a recurring concept or 'residue' of memory. To cement new information, we need to continually adjust and add it to existing mental models; the stronger the colour, the more secure the memory. Where there are gaps, we revisit information regularly through recall, reinforcing the foundations. Such mental structures that correspond to ideas or concepts have been coined 'mental representations' by cognitive psychologist Anders Ericsson (2016). Ericsson's work focuses on acquiring expertise, and mental representations that allow rapid, durable access to information within our memory stores are an integral part of the process.

For knowledge to build, prior knowledge cannot be an assumption; it has to be a certainty. As Sherrington (2017) points out, we need to build schema before we can use them, which is why the development of schema does not happen by chance, but needs to be considered carefully at two key stages: intent (curriculum design) and implementation (whole-school pedagogical practices).

In the classroom, schema-building can be supported through what Arthur Shimamura (2018) calls 'front-loading'. This means introducing pupils to concepts that have already been 'chunked' and organised both visually and spatially, and can be achieved through a range of methods, such as concept maps, schematic representations (such as introducing vocabulary using the Frayer model – see page 159), or the organisation of information through hierarchical structures (for example, a structure following the diagrammatic representation of The Great Chain of Being). Shimamura also insists that learning requires 'top-down processing', in other words, framed through 'big questions' that not only stimulate curiosity but also make explicit connections with the overarching schema. One way to achieve this is to move away from learning objectives that inhibit curiosity towards big questions that inspire enquiry: 'We are learning how to analyse Macbeth's character in the banquet scene' becomes 'How does Macbeth's downfall begin in the banquet scene?' And finally, Shimamura also insists on 'taking stock' of learning at key points to ensure that our pupils are not only 'restating' what they are learning, but 'reframing' it; this is formative assessment with an explicit purpose.

So far, we've understood that making links is integral to schema-building, and should therefore be considered at the heart of curriculum design, but what if the prior knowledge that we are relying on no longer exists; what if that prior knowledge has been forgotten? Here, pedagogical practices come into play during the delivery and implementation phase.

'Learning requires forgetting' (Dylan Wiliam, 2016)

We don't need research to tell us that knowledge no longer revisited can easily be lost in an abyss; however, research certainly helps us to understand how this happens so we can take action to mitigate it. Hermann Ebbinghaus (1850–1909), the first psychologist to systematically study memory and learning, illustrated this through his forgetting curve, a graphical representation of the forgetting process. The key findings? Most of the 'forgetting' occurs within the first hour of learning. By day one to two, we typically forget 75 per cent of what we have learnt. Without any attempts made to revisit, a week later it will be as if the learning never took place in the first instance. There is, however, a point in the curve where the decline levels off, and that is typically around day one to two. Here we can retain some information, essential details, for a few days. This is our window of opportunity. Nuthall, credited with the longest studies into teaching and learning, suggests that it typically takes three encounters with new concepts before 'learning' can take place (2007). The first makes the learner aware, the second allows them to make associations with prior knowledge and the third facilitates embedding the concepts within their retention stores, or 'long-term memory'. This may not be an exact science, but serves as a helpful benchmark. Optimising transfer to 'long-term memory' has therefore been the focus of a significant body of research (Bjork; The Learning Scientists; Dunlosky; Rosenshine).

'Learning is a change in long-term memory' (Tom Sherrington, 2017)

Bjork's (2011) ideas about 'desirable difficulties' focus on maximising 'long-term retention' and propose a range of strategies to challenge our learners to practise accessing their long-term memory stores and retrieve knowledge. After all, how can we know if students have learnt something until they show us that they remember and can apply it? Through carefully guided instruction and planned practices for revisit, recall and retrieval, we can have a significant impact on the retention capacities of our learners. Systematic and spaced review of learning is integral to overcoming the forgetting process, and the first step to ensure this is to begin with our understanding of 'the working memory'.

Putting it into practice

The working memory and cognitive overload

'Any instructional design that flouts or merely ignores working memory limitations is deficient.' John Sweller (1998)

Working memory is finite. It is the opposite of 'long-term memory'. It is the amount of information that can be held in the brain during the processing of cognitive tasks. In the 1950s, it was widely believed that the average working memory could store five to seven items of information; however, recent research identifies this number to be closer to four (Cowan, 2010). Essentially, working memory has restricted bandwidth whereas long-term memory has a huge capacity to store information. Based on this, even the initial task of reading a nineteenth-century text where pupils encounter Tier 2 vocabulary and complex grammatical structures can easily clog up storage, leaving limited capacity to engage with ideas and concepts, which is why 'pre-teaching' or 'flip-learning' or 'front-loading' are as essential to instructional design as the content at the heart of the lesson.

To explain this, Sweller formulated 'cognitive load theory', a theory that Dylan Wiliam once described on Twitter as the 'single most important thing' teachers should know (2017). Storage or central capacity is the bedrock for effective cognitive processing, and it is imperative that both intrinsic and extraneous load is maintained at an optimum level. Intrinsic load is the inherent difficulty associated with a task, whereas working memory load, generated as learners interact with these tasks, is extraneous. Both can be managed through careful planning in the classroom.

Any complex task, such as new information about a topic, or interactivity between existing elements (comparing poems in an anthology), intensifies the intrinsic cognitive load of our learners, so it is incumbent upon us as teachers to minimise their extraneous mental efforts. For example, when introducing a new poem, distributing a selection of worksheets at the same time that focus on different aspects of the learning (context, mark schemes or exemplars), along with a mixture of house-keeping instructions (gluing or hole-punching), immediately intensifies extraneous load and detracts from learning time. On the contrary, providing students with a single sheet (such as a knowledge organiser) or booklet that chunks and sequences information, streamlines the instructional processes and allows pupils to free up mental storage capacities to engage instead with the intrinsic challenges of learning.

Through carefully considered instructional design, we can minimise distractions and manage what is known as the split-attention effect, which comes in two guises:

Spatial contiguity: a diagram with the comparative links between poems on one side but corresponding information on another.

Temporal contiguity: introducing a concept, moving on to instructions about something else (such as an author's visit or competition), before returning to the concept.

It is imperative that we manage the split-attention effect. Learners with low-attention spans remember less when their storage capacity is stretched to hold information that is irrelevant to the assigned task (Cowan, 2010).

One of the most effective ways to manage cognitive load is by making process memories automatic. Think, for instance, about the most common and recurrent processes in the English classroom. An analytical paragraph probably makes it to the top of that list. Moving to Becky Wood's 'What-How-Why' structure for writing analytical paragraphs and away from processes such as PEE, PETER or PETAZL simplifies the process memory design for pupils; they now have a more versatile requisite mental model that can easily be adapted to fit most structures. Repeated use would then create a 'mental representation' within long-term memory, making it easier and more automatic to access and apply this.

To make learning efficient and substantive, we need to continually explore methods that not only make process memories automatic, but also support intrinsic and extraneous mental efforts. For instance, providing students with a structure strip for organising an argument or a speech would ease intrinsic load, while also serving as a process memory tool. Similarly, helping pupils to organise their folders with dividers and labels (based on topics, exam sections or question types) would serve as a process memory tool that will reduce demand on extraneous mental capacities in the long run.

There are of course other methods that reduce cognitive load. We delve into these in detail in this and other chapters, to ensure that they aren't a list to tick through, but carefully considered processing strategies that take centre stage in the English classroom.

Metacognition

In the interest of building mental representations, metacognition is where you hand over the steering wheel. The learner decides when to shift gear, select the best route and employ adaptive measures to overcome any hurdles along the way. In a classroom where metacognitive practices are fostered, the process of accessing and retaining knowledge becomes automatic and proactive for the learner, just like driving a car.

Metacognition is sometimes described as 'thinking about thinking', but is clearly a lot more. It comprises two key components: knowledge about cognition and regulation of that cognition. The first stage is to make the learner aware and reflective of their cognitive processes; the next is to encourage strategic thinking (planning, monitoring and self-regulation). There is a strong correlation between metacognition and academic success, which is why it is rated as one of the most effective strategies by the EEF (2020): 'the equivalent of +7 months' progress when used well'.

Matt Bromley (2018), author and school improvement adviser, identifies six different teaching approaches to support metacognitive thinking, outlined here with some simple strategies that can be incorporated during the curriculum implementation phase.

1. Thinking alone

The goal is to help learners to transition through the four key stages of metacognitive awareness: tacit, aware, strategic, perceptive (Perkins, 1992). Aside from self-reflective exercises, we can do more to extend strategic awareness, sometimes achieved by working backwards:

- Give pupils an exam paper for the first time and ask them to pen down initial thoughts: what does evaluate mean? How long do I have to answer this? How much do I need to write? Once complete, address these 'silent thoughts'.

- Ask pupils to plot grade descriptors in a cloze exercise before sharing the mark scheme. Independent interrogation can stimulate critical thinking and pupils are often accurate in ascribing value and hierarchy. It's also an opportunity to address the nuances between the different modifiers (simple; some; clear; consistent; convincing; compelling) and how they manifest in practice.

2. Thinking together

Guided practice is a precursor to independent practice and Robin Alexander's (2004) seminal work on 'dialogic teaching' provides a pedagogical framework for this. According to the EEF, Alexander's 'learning talk' (narrating, questioning and discussing) and 'teaching talk' (instruction, exposition and dialogue) are effective repertoires for developing metacognitive skills.

- Use 'I do, we do, you do', based on Rosenshine's (2012) pedagogy, to live model challenging tasks. Don't be afraid to discuss contributions that don't fit. Normalise redrafting.

- Use reciprocal reading strategies to interrogate challenging texts. With explicit instructions and sustained practice, pupils will be able to complete this independently, without prompts.

3. Thinking efficiently

Thinking efficiently is essential to overcoming the limitations of working memory, and can be achieved if learners have a repertoire of metacognitive strategies at their disposal. Talk to pupils about cognitive overload, and then provide supportive scaffolds that can be encoded as procedural knowledge. The only caveat? Strategic instruction works in tandem with secure background knowledge, which requires continued development through 'deep content exploration' (Willingham and Lovette, 2014).

- Organise the categorisation of physical and digital folders, and then encourage access. For instance, for a descriptive task, direct pupils to the 'creative writing' section of their folder to use previously shared scaffolds for planning, vocabulary or structure. The more they revisit 'physical' knowledge stores, the easier it becomes to activate knowledge in long-term memory, and the more secure their links.

- Create a 'strategy wall' in the classroom with an array of scaffolds categorised by topic and/or skills (planning; structuring an argument; narrative writing). Initially, guide the selection process before moving towards autonomous selection. To take notes, pupils might benefit from the Cornell note-taking method (a systematic note-taking strategy devised by education professor, Walter Pauk); to write an argument, a pre-prepared structure strip (created by primary teacher @mrlockyer and adapted for secondary English by @MrsSpalding) might be helpful; and for comparing two poems, try a fishbone diagram (also known as an Ishikawa diagram), which, although devised as a cause-and-effect analysis tool by Professor Kaoru Ishikawa, is equally supportive as a visualisation strategy for finding common threads. Giving autonomy to select the most appropriate scaffold and allowing pupils to make mistakes is integral to fostering metacognitive thinking.

4. Thinking aloud

The learner is a novice and you are the expert; make explicit the complexity of your thinking and make explicit what you do implicitly.

- During live modelling, narrate your thought process: 'I am choosing to do question 3 before question 2 because…'; 'I have created a Tier 2 vocabulary bank so that I can make my argument more compelling when I discuss…'

- Use technology to give audio feedback. Audio recordings are easy to insert in most programmes. Scan a piece of work and record a voice-over as you mark, explaining your annotations and suggesting improvements. Frame your suggestions with questions: 'How can we develop this idea further? Here is what I would do…'

5. Thinking hard

To encode information in long-term memory, pupils need to be challenged to activate, retrieve or make connections with prior knowledge. In other words, 'desirable difficulty', as coined by Bjork (1994) in his seminal work on memory, is thus a necessary condition for learning.

- Ask pupils to submit an essay plan with an audio recording that articulates their thought processes. According to research, 'self-explanation' and 'elaboration' are highly effective practices (Sumeracki, 2020).

- Turn the pupil into the master. Share a range of exemplars, show examiner analysis videos and ask pupils to annotate like an examiner would. Scaffold this through the provision of grade-specific descriptors, such as 'clear explanation of effect'; 'thoughtful inference'; and 'perceptive comparison'.

6. Thinking positively

Research suggests that when gratification is delayed, pupils are more efficient at planning and self-regulation. Pupils need to be taught to delay their gratification and develop self-motivation skills instead. This motivation comes in two guises: intrinsic and extrinsic. Extrinsic motivation can be influenced with rewards or sanctions, whereas intrinsic motivation stems from an inherent desire to learn, to challenge and to do better. Begin with the former to foster the latter; help learners make connections and contextualise their learning to see the point of it all.

- Encourage pupils to enter competitions, creating avenues for the acknowledgement and celebration of ideas and efforts.

- For writing tasks, bring in real audiences and purposes (this is also covered in Chapter 5). For example, ask pupils to write to their local MP and present an argument around an issue that matters to them.

Knowledge organisers

Knowledge organisers set out important, useful and powerful knowledge on any given topic on a single page. They are effective resources that allow pupils to both retain and retrieve information needed for their studies. Before creating knowledge organisers, it is useful to think about three keys areas: purpose, content and presentation.

The purpose of knowledge organisers is to ensure the correct knowledge is learnt, retained and retrieved by pupils. Using a pre-made knowledge organiser should therefore be treated with caution. Does it contain the information needed for the curriculum journey you have designed? Consideration of the learning journey here is key. Content also plays an important role in their design. Powerful knowledge, as defined by Michael Young and Johan Muller (2013), in their article 'On the powers of powerful knowledge', is specialised rather than general knowledge. Therefore, the choice about what to include needs careful consideration. What do you want pupils to learn? How will this knowledge develop them as learners and citizens? Finally, consideration should be made of how pupils will be assessed at the end of the unit. Presentation on the organisers is also an important factor. Many organisers list information and have separate sections for each subsection of information. This can be useful for retrieval practice, but also consider the need for the information to link together in some way. The design of the page should suit the way in which the information will be referred to throughout the teaching of the unit.

Once you have created a knowledge organiser, it's time to put it to good use in the classroom. There are a few ways this can take place.

A deeper level of knowledge is needed for pupils to develop strong knowledge. Effective elaboration opportunities of the content on the knowledge organiser supports this aim: connecting ideas, in-depth discussion and the explicit teaching of further content all help to solidify knowledge in the long-term memory. When pupils return to the knowledge organiser regularly, these elaborations are also recalled, deepening their knowledge. Willingham (2014) espouses that this kind of elaborative interrogation must contain active understanding and meaningful consideration of what is being learnt.

Retrieval practice is an effective way of making sure the knowledge is returned to frequently. Low-stakes retrieval quizzing ensures the content is stored in the long-term memory and retrieved at regular intervals. This can be done by filling in the blanks, creating timelines or focusing on one key area on the knowledge organiser.

Another effective use of a knowledge organiser is to ask pupils to reorganise the information in some way. The more the pupils synthesise the knowledge, the more likely they are to remember it. By reordering the information using activities like ranking, connecting themes and ideas, and presenting it differently, students are transferring it to their long-term memory and therefore stand a better chance of remembering the information.

Dual coding

Dual coding is a way of organising information so that pupils gain a better chance of not only understanding it on first reception, when information first enters the working memory, but also when returned to, as stronger connections are formed that enable long-term memory storage and retrieval. Dual coding is a process whereby written or verbal materials are accompanied by visuals. It works by taking advantage of two channels for processing information. When our working memory receives new information, the channels by which we receive them, such as visual or auditory, are stored in different areas. By using both visual and auditory stimuli for the same topic, it increases the likelihood of it being remembered.

There are many visual stimuli ideas you could include alongside verbal and written information. Some of these have been included below:

- **Icons:** coupled with key concepts, these work really well to ensure pupils understand the meaning behind abstract ideas.

- **Graphs:** useful for exploring the stages of a narrative, like Freytag's pyramid, for example. They also work well when tracking the rise and fall of emotions across a text, like tension, for example.

- **Timelines:** these work well when placing texts within a time frame plotted against other texts that you teach. They allow pupils to make temporal connections between the texts that lead to a greater understanding of each individual text and their possible influences.

- **Infographics:** these work well for summarising information and condensing knowledge into its constituent parts.

- **Images:** used in the exam papers for the creative writing section, these can work as useful prompts when helping pupils to decide upon their narrative content, but they are also equally useful when explaining things more generally in the English classroom.

- **Maps:** these are fantastic for exploring contextual information about a time period of a text students are studying. For example, Charles Booth's London poverty maps are a brilliant way to explore the streets that

> Dickens walked: the very source of influence that feeds into his delightful texts. Students are able to see the scale of the poverty visually and understand how that may have impacted Dickens's life as well as his writing.

It's important to remember both spatial contiguity and temporal contiguity when creating resources and planning for their delivery in the English classroom to avoid any cognitive overload for our pupils. Another imperative point is that once you have decided upon a particular visual for the substantive knowledge you wish to embed, it would be best to stick to that visual during the first learning episodes before possibly moving on to synthesise this during revision lessons. This allows consideration for any extraneous mental capacities and the split-attention effect. The key is to ensure all learners are successful.

Live modelling

Think about the times when you use your satnav to navigate to any new destination. The route is unfamiliar, so your attention is split between following instructions and observations (intrinsic load). Your working memory will presumably be close to full capacity if you are also thinking about transient factors, such as road signs or restrictions, or focusing on your intended destination and what will happen on arrival (split-attention effect). If someone then asks you to replicate your journey or retrace your steps without detailed instructions, chances are that you will probably miss a turn.

This understanding is key when you embark on live modelling in the classroom; despite carefully guided instruction at every step, there is a risk of cognitive overload. Here are some measures that you can take to ensure that extraneous strains on central capacity are curtailed during the modelling process, and that by the end of it, your students are left with a blueprint of the road map that they can replicate with confidence. When live modelling is done well, incorporating dialogic talk and metacognitive practices, not only will pupils know what to do to move from point A to B, but they will also be able to articulate how and why.

Tips for successful live modelling

1. Talk through your preliminary thinking; narrate the process of how you construct a plan of action and explain your reasoning:
   'How would I approach this unseen poem? Here's what I will want to do first because…'
2. Keep diversions in instructions to a minimum to avoid spatial or temporal contiguity. Only fill working memory with the essentials. Only make links that reinforce patterns and develop schema:
   'We will use the same framework for comparison that we used when we…'
3. Model each stage, but frame it, contextualise it and signpost it. Think of these signposts as physical signs along any journey. We need to know about the postbox and billboard at the corner if we are expected to memorise and retrace our steps. Chunk the process into neat little categories: highlighting key words; selecting evidence; making links; identifying patterns; numbering points.
4. Give abstract concepts concrete frameworks and then give them a name to refer back to. To see an example of such mental representations in practice, see Zara Shah's talk on metacognition for the 'number line' approach to evaluation: https://t.co/1I3iGjswFd?amp=1

5. Don't present one route; talk about choices. Again, frame these carefully so they don't overwhelm but encourage proactive decision-making:
'I have four pieces of evidence that I can use to analyse this, but I am not going to start with the first one I have highlighted. Why not?'

Once you have established a task-dependent route or framework, revisit and reapply this to a range of different contexts and tasks for successful encoding. After all, the point of live modelling is that you help students transition from guided to independent practice as swiftly and securely as possible.

Interleaving and spacing

Together, interleaving and spacing work as learning methods to ensure the wonderful, knowledge-rich content and skills taught in the English classroom are stored in the long-term memory of your pupils and retrieved when needed. Crucial to their understanding is the previously mentioned work by Ebbinghaus and the forgetting curve (see page 174). Interleaving and spacing are both methods which, when planned carefully, can move pupils' learning along effectively. Each of them is explained below.

Interleaving is a powerful learning method from which all pupils will benefit in the English classroom. It involves switching between topics through a planned learning journey in order for the knowledge to transfer to the long-term memory and, therefore, the most effective learning takes place. In the English classroom, this works best when running English language and English literature alongside one another or as combined units rather than as stand alone units or blocks of work. The topics being interleaved are best planned with some conceptual connections in mind and, as such, this should be considered a very useful tool when designing an English curriculum. By creating an interleaved curriculum, you ensure that any links, similarities or differences between topics and skills are clear. New information is much more likely to stick in the long-term memory as a result. So, what does this look like in practice? Let's take a literature topic such as *Macbeth*, for example, and the language topic of non-fiction reading. Instead of having them as stand alone units that are not connected in any way, pupils could be expected to read an article on witchcraft as part of their study of the contextual information underpinning *Macbeth*. The units are interleaved and blended to allow the pupils' minds to forge better connections. As already mentioned, research tells us this type of learning works best.

Spacing involves the careful planning of content that is returned to throughout a learning journey or curriculum map. When considering what knowledge and skills pupils should learn and when they should learn it, spacing is key. It forms the route through your curriculum and the ultimate success of the pupils' learning journey. Taking the example above, the unit on *Macbeth* forms a small part in a much larger planned curriculum. Questions to consider are: how much Shakespeare knowledge do pupils have before they begin to learn about *Macbeth*? At what point do pupils begin to learn about non-fiction reading and the skills required to master this topic? Certainly, in this example, pupils would have accumulated knowledge of Shakespeare spaced across each key stage or even year group and one would expect non-fiction reading skills to have already been covered earlier in the curriculum too. This is where careful spacing works best. Knowing when and where to space particular knowledge and teaching of skills is vital to ensuring pupils are given the best possible chance of success.

Retrieval practice

In any well-planned, knowledge-rich curriculum, you are going to cover an impressive amount of content. This content will be required for pupils to achieve the best possible academic success. Bjork tells us that retrieval works best as a recall and memory modifier (Bjork, 1988). It goes without saying then that we must ensure our pupils are able to retrieve, synthesise and make new connections with the information they have retained. Retrieval practice is a powerful learning tool to achieve this aim. Notable benefits for teachers are that it enables you to identify gaps in knowledge and address misconceptions. Pupils also benefit from better organisation and increased confidence as a result of being successful. Retrieval practice involves the consistent retrieval of learnt information across a curriculum journey. It's been a buzzword in education in recent years, with many educators advocating its success in their classrooms. The practice lends itself nicely to the English classroom as our brilliant subject is full of conceptual links. Its success relies upon it being low stakes and well thought through. Done well, it reaps benefits for our pupils.

There are many different ways to include retrieval practice in lessons. Some of the best suited to the English classroom are listed below.

- **Multiple-choice quiz:** a firm favourite of many teachers, this approach works best where there are only three possible answers to choose from: one correct answer, one nuanced incorrect answer and one incorrect answer. This makes the task accessible for all pupils without the negation of challenge for the more able learners.

- **Summarising:** a simple retrieval task involving pupils summarising the information they learned last lesson, week, term or year. This can be done using specified template designs to support all learners or as a free recall.

- **Free recall:** the classic brain dump to assess where students are with their learning. Pupils write down everything they can remember about a certain topic.

- **Timelines:** asking pupils to place things in order helps to encode memory. Plotting events in a text, the chronology of texts studied, the order in which characters appear and so on are all useful retrieval tasks.

- **Prompts:** images or icons used to trigger recall work well, particularly for pupils with English as an additional language.

It's worth noting that retrieval practice does have pitfalls. These usually occur as a result of poor task design; too much time thinking about the task rather than the questions you want answered; not planning enough time for feedback and reflection; a heavy reliance on factual recall alone; and getting the desirable difficulty of the task just right. Research on retrieval practice is abundant and well worth studying.

Walking talking mocks

Walking talking mocks have become a popular revision strategy amongst many educators in recent years. Underpinned by metacognition research theories, they are an effective way of ensuring pupils understand the thinking process behind the questions in the exams they are required to sit. Their aim is to solidify exam knowledge and skill as well as perform successfully on the day itself. Like the analogy shared at the beginning of this chapter, the teacher is effectively steering the pupils in the right direction, so when it is their turn to take the wheels, they are not only ready, but successful.

So, how do they work? Pupils sit in the hall where they would take their final exams, but instead of simply allowing them to sit the paper as they would traditionally do, the teacher walks them through each question step by step. Walking talking mocks work best when pupils sit in the seats they would sit in for the real exam and the paper they are revising from is in the same form as the real thing. Here is a handy process to consider when conducting one:

1. **Command words:** every question has these. They essentially instruct the pupils to answer the question using a certain skill. For example, the word 'retrieve' involves the skill of sourcing information from a text, whereas the word 'analyse' involves understanding writer's choices and interpreting language choices. In a walking talking mock, the teacher will identify these words, annotate them and explain their importance to the question.

2. **Annotations:** as the process is taking place, the teacher will be annotating their own copy of the exam paper with notes about command words, possible ways in which to respond and brief content ideas that may be covered.

3. **Visualiser:** it's also important that as the teacher is talking pupils through the process and modelling the annotations, pupils are able to see what they are writing and can replicate the process on their own paper at the same time.

4. **Thinking aloud:** at all times, the teacher should be verbalising the thought process that goes into

understanding the questions and the possible approaches to answering.

Once you and your lovely pupils have grown accustomed to this way of revising, walking talking mocks become such a useful revision tool. As an aside, they double up resourcefully on days when you may need to plan something quickly for a year group due to unforeseen circumstances (like a global pandemic causing your entire English team to be absent!).

Feedback for marginal gains

'The only thinking that matters is what the student does with the feedback.' Dylan Wiliam (2016)

If you ask a toddler to clean their room, the desired results will be variable. Presumably lacking both the intrinsic motivation as well as the procedural knowledge, they may not know where to begin. They may feel overwhelmed with the high expectations, ignore you completely, or start but get distracted along the way, since the task assigned is beyond their expertise.

Instead, if you guide the child in stages, instructing them to put the crayons away in the green box, and then the dinosaurs away in the blue, you have a stronger chance of achieving your desired goal. This is David Brailsford's theory about marginal gains in practice, where marginal gains aggregate towards a bigger goal and outcome. Quite simply, chunking tasks into manageable and specific actions allows for small, incremental improvements; it makes the impossible seem possible. After all, you don't need to see the whole staircase to take that first step, as the saying goes.

Let's contextualise this within an English classroom. 'Be more perceptive to move to the next level' may be honest and accurate feedback, but it won't get the desired outcome if being 'perceptive' is beyond the learner's skill set. To a learner, feedback beyond their current state of expertise can be as overwhelming as the task to clean the room when you don't know how or where to begin. Instead, substituting the aspirational goal with short, specific and achievable actions just might do the trick. Feedback, when done right, is central to learning and is ranked as one of the most effective strategies to accelerate progress (EEF). For feedback to be effective, it must focus on future performance rather than the past (Sherrington and Caviglioli, 2020). Dylan Wiliam calls this 'responsive teaching', where feedback moves the learning along the learning cycle, activating pupils as owners of their own learning.

Feedback for marginal gains focuses on building self-efficacy, rather than self-esteem, a key feature of metacognitive practice; learners are trained not to feel good about themselves, but good about what they can do. Bandura's work demonstrates that when we focus on self-efficacy, accomplishments are more stable, robust and feed forward into future endeavours.

Driven by this rationale, Figures 8.1 and 8.2 offer examples of two 'feedback for progress' proformas designed by teachers Kerry Kurczij and Zara Shah at The Grammar School at Leeds (2019).

Teachers use these proforma throughout the learning cycle, focusing on formative actions instead of summative numbers. They highlight two to three actionable targets in different colours, and use the corresponding colours to identify where the work needs to be adapted. The use of colour acts as a clear, visual prompt, reducing cognitive load and focusing attention to the immediate next steps in the learning. The feedback is explicit and supportive, acting as stabilisers and giving pupils the gentle push they need to make secure improvements in both knowledge and performance, so they can replicate these actions independently in the future.

GSAL English Department CheckPoint Challenge
KS3 Feedback for Progress Reading

Marks: A02   +   –   =   n/a   /8

Task-related strengths	Task-related targets

Recipe for future action
1. **Rewrite** this paragraph/section using the What-How-Why structure
2. **Plan** this task again to answer the question more precisely.
3. **Add** one further new point to your answer: *'Furthermore, the writer also ...'*
4. **Insert** quotations to support your point here: *'This is evident in the quotation...'*
5. **Edit/embed** your quotation where signalled.
6. **Contextualise** the evidence: *'This is evident when... revealed in the quotation...'*
7. **Unpack** the language used in this quotation: *'The word ... has connotations of...'*
8. **Insert** language/literary term here: *'The use of [insert technique] highlights...'*
9. **Provide** an alternative interpretation here: *'Perhaps ...could also suggest...'*
10. **Develop** your analysis: *'Moreover, the use of ... also highlights...'*
11. **Explore** patterns: *'The repeated use of a range of...'; 'The semantic field of...'*
12. **Explain** the impact/effects in a clear and specific manner: *'makes the reader visualise just how...', 'creating an atmosphere of...'*
13. **Link** back to the focus of the question: *'therefore reinforcing that...'*
14. **Other:**

GSAL English Department CheckPoint Challenge
KS3 Feedback for Progress Writing

Marks: A05   /12   +   –   =   n/a   A06:   /8

Task related strengths	Task related Targets

Recipe for future action
1. **Correct** the accuracy errors signalled.
2. **Rewrite** your opening/ending to better achieve:
3. **Plan** this task again making a priority of creating a strong structure.
4. **Write** a chronological list of improved topic sentences.
5. **Insert** discourse markers to better show links between points and the development of the content: *'Moreover; Furthermore; Similarly; In contrast.'*
6. **Elevate** your vocabulary choices/expression here.
7. **Engineer** more sentence variety here (using 'The Sentences Pack' for help).
8. **Adapt** style and register here for audience and purpose.
9. **Use** more sophisticated punctuation here for deliberate effect : ; - ( ) ' '
10. **Rewrite** this section using 'show, don't tell.'
11. **Edit** this section to include more figurative language/rhetorical devices
12. **Develop** your description/ ideas/ reasons/ logos/ ethos/ pathos at this point.
13. **Link** back to your line of argument
14. **Other:**

FIGURE 8.1 *Feedback for progress proforma for Key Stage 3 reading and writing*

Language Paper 2 Section A Qs 4
AO4 Comparing writers'...
- Ideas
- Perspectives
- Methods

Level	Marks	Comparisons of POV	Evidence	Analysis of methods
4	16 15 14 13	PC Detailed and perceptive comparison of different POVs [ideas and perspectives]	Judiciously selected and a range of supporting evidence from both texts	PE Analysis of writers' methods and their effects
3	12 11 10 9	CC Clear comparison of the different POVs	Clear and relevant supporting evidence from both texts	CE Clear explanation of writers' methods and their effects
2	8 7 6 5	AC Some attempts to compare different POVs	Some appropriate references/ evidence from one or both texts	AE Attempts to comment on methods and their effects

Level:	**Recipe for future action**
	1. **Rewrite** using the What-How-Why structure
	2. **Recraft** so that your point is focused on the POV / tone / idea / perspective / question
Mark:	3. **Insert / embed** evidence here
	4. **Contextualise** the evidence: *'This is evident when...'; 'and revealed in the quotation...'*
	5. **Unpack** the language used here: *'The word ... has connotations of / makes you think of...'*
	6. **Zoom** in on the writer's use of methods: *'The use of [insert technique] highlights...'*
	7. **Develop** your analysis here: *'Moreover, the use of ... also implies ...'*
+ - =	8. **Provide** an alternative and perceptive inference here: *'Perhaps...' 'might also suggest...'*
	9. **Explore** patterns: *'The repeated use of a range of...'; 'The semantic field of...'*
	10. **Explain** the impact / effects in a clear and specific manner: *'creates an impression of...';* *'makes the reader visualise / appreciate just how...'; 'building an atmosphere / feeling of...'*
	11. **Link** back to the POV: *'therefore reinforcing how the writer...'; 'making it clear why the* *writer...'; 'reiterating just how...'; 'the writer would have...'*
	12. **Insert** comparative discourse markers: *'On the other hand...'; 'Similarly...'; 'Conversely...'*
	13. **Analyse** a wider range of subject terminology: *'Moreover, the writer also uses...'*
	14. **Other:**

Confidence rating for this question:

1   2   3   4   5   6   7   8   9   10

One aspect that I am still unsure about is:

FIGURE 8.2 *Feedback for progress proforma for GCSE English language*

Whatever the shape that feedback takes, it is important to avoid what Caviglioli and Sherrington (date unknown) describe as the 'satnav' syndrome. Our focus is not to get our pupils from point A to B without an awareness of how they arrived, but give them a road map that allows them to articulate, replicate and retrace their steps. Only then can we cultivate an 'ethic of excellence' (Berger, 2003), where carefully guided instruction and support is used to ensure that 'excellence' is within the grasp of all of our pupils.

Summary

- Study the science of learning. It has provided a greater understanding of how pupils learn. Start with a book like *Why Don't Students Like School?* by Daniel Willingham (2009) before moving on to more academically heavy research papers.
- The research, methods and ideas explored in this chapter are effective in boosting pupils' knowledge, but they are not exhaustive and, like all great things, they will evolve.
- Stay engaged with current research as an active, ever-evolving educator. Use Twitter to look out for new edubooks and keep an eye on academic sites like JSTOR for research papers.

9

Revision

*Abigail Mann and
Laura May Rowlands*

Introduction

Before we begin this short chapter, it is worth mentioning that a well-planned curriculum will have in-built consolidation points and a scheme that ensures revision of content takes place throughout the year. Any last-minute attempt to revise huge amounts of content is unlikely to be successful without such a curriculum in place. That said, effective revision strategies can be handy when the run-up to exams is upon you and we all know the best type of revision lessons are structured ones (long gone are the ineffective, independent revision lessons where pupils made useless, but very pretty, posters that served no purpose). This chapter offers you a handful of methods for consolidation and retrieval of content in the English classroom that should be used in conjunction with, not as opposed to, many teaching methods already mentioned earlier in the book. They can be built into schemes of learning throughout the year or in the run-up to the all-important exams at the end of a course. These ideas are underpinned by research already discussed in Chapter 8, The science of learning. As such, we shall get stuck straight in with the content.

Putting it into practice

Blank knowledge organisers

One way to reduce stress for pupils in the run-up to the exams is to get them to check what they do and don't know. Enter: the blank knowledge organiser. This is a great way of checking what pupils don't need to spend more time on and what they need to focus on. Ask pupils to undertake this activity weekly during the revision season for maximum impact.

So, how does it work? Ask pupils to take a look at their populated knowledge organiser. It should be grouped into several columns with different headings, as set out by the teacher. Ask pupils to recreate the outline of this on a blank piece of paper. They should use a ruler if they need to. Now, ask them to time themselves for five minutes to try and 'populate' the boxes. If they need to, they can leave some blank – that will be their first clue about what has made it into their long-term memory.

Next, this is the step which may hurt their pride. Ask pupils to use a different coloured pen for this. Using your original knowledge organiser, fill in the blank sections of the knowledge organiser they just tried to recreate. Let's say they used a black pen at first, then filled in the blanks with a green pen. The black pen work is all of the knowledge they have secured in their long-term memory – it's important to ask pupils to revisit this as part of their revision, but this isn't what needs work. The section in green pen should be their focus for that week. This process should be repeated weekly until all of the knowledge from the populated knowledge organiser has been secured.

Going forward, ask pupils to keep hold of their weekly blank knowledge organisers as a way of motivating them to keep going. If they are focusing on the right information from week to week, the amount of green should decrease! This will boost their confidence and decrease their stress levels.

Complex mind maps

Mind maps are a visual creation that presents or outlines information on any given topic. Mind mapping is an effective revision tool as it allows pupils to retrieve declarative knowledge from the long-term memory and to organise their thoughts clearly on the page. They have been used in education for many years, but when completed without direction or planning, pupils can often fall short of achieving their purpose. Complex mind maps are planned carefully by the teacher so that pupils' memories are prompted and connections made upon retrieval. They are a powerful revision tool that can be returned to time and again. In the English classroom, they lend themselves nicely to English literature and substantive knowledge of the texts studied.

So, where should you begin with revision mind maps? Well, it would be best to create a template which pupils can then work on. Firstly, start in the middle with the topic you are revising. This will form the central basis from which all other information will stem. Secondly, the branches that stem from the main idea should detail the key themes or strands that connect to the central topic or idea. Finally, from these branches, any other relevant and key ideas should be labelled. It is essentially a spider's web of connected ideas that pupils need to remember in order to revise successfully for that particular topic. This complex planning should see your pupils creating effective mind maps in no time.

It's important to note that mind maps are most effective when coupled with dual coding of some description. There are many variations that you could try with your pupils. Couple images with words to help trigger memory, for example. In addition, some pupils prefer to use symbols and keys to connect their ideas together, and to help them to retain important information in a more memorable way. Once this coding is taking place, it enables further opportunity to recall knowledge by using images, symbols and icons alone, and asking pupils to write down the relevant text and so on. Mind maps are also a resource that can be returned to throughout a revision period in order to add further knowledge. They become powerful working documents in any revision episode and are a worthy activity in any English classroom.

Effective elaboration

This idea was shared by Rebeka Aylwin, sociology teacher and head of the humanities faculty at Oriel High School. It is an effective revision strategy in the English classroom due to our heavy substantive knowledge base.

A common barrier to effective revision for many pupils is that they don't know what they don't know. Encouraging pupils to assess their knowledge and understanding through testing themselves can take a range of formats. Elaboration is a great starting point for pupils to highlight their areas of strength and to also move out of their revision comfort zone, to focus on their areas of weakness.

Pupils should begin with their notes to hand. Having prompts to form the foundation of their revision session ensures they have a starting block to build upon, which helps to break the intimidation of a blank page. Remembering that practice doesn't just make perfect, it also makes permanent, pupils must use their notes to make sure they are remembering the correct information.

Prompts give the bare bones from which to start their elaboration and should be broken down into small and manageable chunks of information. Some effective prompts include:

- key vocabulary mats
- diagrams or graphs
- illustrations
- a copy of the syllabus
- personalised learning checklists
- topic sentences
- exam questions.

From this point, there are a number of ways you can use elaboration to build knowledge and understanding.

Step 1

A simple way to begin is with a 'brain dump'. Using the prompts, pupils list or mind map anything they can remember about a particular topic, in no specific order. This uncomplicated strategy means they can just focus on getting their ideas on paper and this information can then be developed with further elaboration activities. At this point, encourage pupils to check their notes and make corrections and additions of anything they've left out. Using a different coloured pen to do so can help to highlight the parts that are more of a challenge to remember. Doing this activity a few times should help to improve recall until they are able to retain the majority of the information on a topic.

Step 2

Urge pupils to go beyond recall, deepening their understanding of the topic by asking questions, and lots of them. Giving them a list of question stems that escalate in difficulty can ensure the information they revise is digested by using their higher-order thinking skills. This could be done independently as a written activity, or verbally as a paired activity. For example:

- Who was...?
- What are the features of...?
- Why did X happen?
- When did...?
- What caused...?
- How can you explain...?
- What happens when...?
- What could be different if...?
- What changes would you make to solve...?
- Can you predict the outcome if...?

Step 3

Pupils can develop their elaboration activities further by building connections between ideas on the same topic. One way to do this is to get them to randomly pick two ideas from their prompt list and draw a table with the headings 'similarities' and 'differences'. The advice given on how to do this will be very context bound, but pupils can be encouraged to think of all of the factors that these ideas, concepts, theories or events have in common with each other, and what makes them stand out. The more pupils can add connections and details, the deeper their learning.

Step 4

Another way of making connections is through our own experiences, either through past memory or day-to-day life.

Prior learning and encounters can teach pupils of categories and concrete examples, which can provide the glue for understanding and in-depth learning. Getting pupils to make associations of information in their short-term working memory with information that is already in their long-term memory can help to create 'hooks'. These hooks help to strengthen connections in their memory, organise ideas, produce explanations and bring information to the front of their minds more easily. Encourage pupils to think about where they may have experienced something similar and where they may see what they are learning in real life. You can also guide pupils to make these connections by modelling concrete examples in your own life. By doing this, pupils are essentially connecting newer information to embedded knowledge, and integrating new material into their long-term memory.

Once pupils are confident practitioners in elaboration, they should work their way towards revising without their prompt material, whilst also remembering to check the information in their class notes or with their teacher. Ensure that pupils do not over complicate their elaborations but use them instead to build connections between information to strengthen the pathways in their memories. Elaboration can be a challenging revision activity as it requires us to think about information in a range of different ways. One reminder that it is helpful to give pupils at this point is that the bits where they really struggle are also the ones where they are learning the most.

5, 4, 3, 2, 1

This is a simple revision strategy that relies upon knowledge retrieval of previously taught content. It works best when spaced retrieval and interleaving are considered (see page 188). As such, it can be done at the start of a revision lesson or as part of a longer-term scheme of learning throughout the year. The aim of the learning episode is to retrieve specific information as instructed by the teacher.

An example of how this might look is below.

Example

Group: Year 10
Unit: *A Christmas Carol* revision
Topic: Scrooge

5 – List five facts about the character of Scrooge in *A Christmas Carol*.
4 – List four themes that Dickens presents through the character of Scrooge.
3 – Write down three quotations that connect Scrooge to the concept of avarice.
2 – Write down two interpretations or layers of meaning for one of the quotations.
1 – Create a topic sentence that connects Scrooge to the concept of avarice.

With the example above, what pupils are beginning to do is to create connections in their mind between information they may have been taught across several different lessons as part of a much bigger journey. By using this task at the beginning of a lesson, it sets them up nicely to begin to think about answering an exam question on Scrooge as a construct. The final task of creating a topic sentence actually hinges nicely on the expectation that pupils write an analytical essay in the exams. It therefore becomes the starting point of such a task, while the other tasks in the activity provide the basis for more content to be used in the essay.

The example above is just one way of retrieving knowledge in a revision lesson. The variations that can be made here are plentiful, and careful consideration into the aims of the revision lesson or activity are key. This activity can be repeated and adapted slightly each time to allow pupils to synthesise knowledge and forge stronger connections that will enable in-depth retrieval as time goes on. It's a powerful and versatile tool once the planning and thought process have been mastered by the teacher.

Essay plans

When it comes to revising for exams in the English classroom, the content of the literature texts studied can often seem overwhelming to pupils, and that's unsurprising given the amount of time and in-depth knowledge you have taught over the two-year GCSE or A level course. Of course, we want our pupils to be given the wonderful joy that is a knowledge-rich curriculum, but the tricky part for some pupils is trying to retrieve this information and apply it to exam questions. Essay plans are a useful way for pupils to prepare for this eventuality. Essentially, they are templates that pupils can populate, revise from and return to over time in order to add or retrieve useful knowledge.

So, how do you include them in an effective revision schedule? Well, there are many ways in which this can happen, but it would be wise to combine both direct instruction and modelling in the first instance. If we want our pupils to create effective essay plans, we need to first show them how.

There are variations on how to create essay plans, but a blank essay template might typically include three columns that address a possible response to an exam question:

1. **What?** What does the writer tell us about this question? What is important?

2. **How?** How does the writer tell us this? How do key words and phrases help to show us this?

3. **Why?** Why is the writer telling us this? Why might they want us to know this? Why might a reader or audience react differently when the text was first written, to how we might react now?

On first attempts at this during revision-teaching, and by using direct instruction and modelling, the teacher is able to create a detailed and effective essay plan that pupils can then use as a model for further independent revision. As the revision lessons continue, using 'I do, we do, you do' as an approach allows pupils to become efficient and competent enough to complete the task alone.

The templates become versatile too. As time goes on, the way in which you ask pupils to recall could be changed. For example, the 'what' column could be populated by the teacher, and pupils are required to fill in the 'how' and 'why' columns. This task retrieval then works on a rotation to ensure that no knowledge is left behind and, by process of interleaving, retrieval is repeated, forming more secure long-term memory storage.

Chanting for success

This idea was contributed by Claire Thompson, assistant headteacher at Whitefield School. It adopts strategies that have been utilised for hundreds of years on the terraces of sporting arenas and in the meditative mantras of a yoga session. Couple this with the incessant repetition of an earworm, and you have the recipe for recall in high-pressure, high-stress situations – exams!

Singing in unison at football matches develops a collective sense that anything is possible for the team the fans are singing for. The songs – catchy words of encouragement and praise – are designed to lift spirits and celebrate successes. And they are designed to do so in arenas of the highest expectation, highest scrutiny and highest pressure. The more the song is sung, the more the words and the intention become second nature; this is the very essence of what we are trying to achieve in the high pressure of an exam hall.

Calming and grounding, mantras in yoga are used to focus the mind and create greater concentration on what processes and information occupy our brains in the present moment. This present moment could be the moment a curve-ball question is discovered in an exam, rendering minds blank and thoughts chaotic. What better tool to have at your disposal than the ability to calm your mind and rely on a well-rehearsed mantra?

Earworms, those infuriating songs that pop into your head at the least opportune moments, can be tiresome. However, it is believed that earworms are more likely to play themselves on repeat during times of greatest stress. For our wonderful pupils, this may very well be during exams. So, why not plant some earworms in the hope that they will indeed rear their heads, just as stress does the same?

Combining these three tried and tested methods leads to the revision essentials of chanting for success. The chanting itself has three different purposes – addressing misconceptions, embedding exam structures and motivating pupils for success – but each is designed to support pupils in either their retention and recall, or their motivation and resilience.

So, how does this all work? First, think of the reason for a chant.

For example, when addressing a **misconception**, the following chant could be used:

'I will not use apostrophes to indicate plurals.'

And an example for addressing **exam skills**, in this case imaginative writing structure:

'Setting, shift, zoom in, zoom out.'

Finally, a chant that can be used as a **motivator** for success:

'Rain hard; fight easy!'

Once you have chosen the chant, you must establish it with the pupils. There are a number of ways that you can do this, but modelling the chant first is essential. The two most effective ways are to ask pupils to repeat what you have said, or make associations with key triggers. For example:

'Say it with me, "I must use a topic sentence to introduce a paragraph."'

'When I say "repetition," you say "emphasis".'

Don't worry if you are a little unsure about beginning the chanting activity. Start small and use one or two words as practice. It's amazing how quickly the pupils get on board and the atmosphere in the room really is exciting yet purposeful. Before you know it, you'll have many classes happily chanting for success and dare I say it, you might even enjoy it yourself.

Summary

- Build revision activities into your schemes of learning, and curriculum maps as regular retrieval points. Retrieval practice in each lesson is a great way to revise previous content.
- Ensure the science of learning underpins your revision strategies. Use interleaving and spaced retrieval when designing revision activities and your schemes of learning.
- Ensure you identify gaps and misconceptions and re-teach the knowledge for these gaps. Low-stakes quizzing, questioning and retrieval activities will support you in identifying these gaps.

10

Becoming a head of department

Ruth Holder and Andy Sammons

Introduction

A head of English is a key middle manager in any school and provides a link between teachers and SLT; alongside the head of maths, this role is essentially the engine room of success in the school. It is the place where ethos, values and curriculum principles are articulated into concrete plans that provide structure, clarity and direction for teachers so that schools can give young people the education they deserve.

Just some of the day-to-day responsibilities when taking on such a role include decision-making, curriculum development, organisation of classes, timetabling, and line management of post-holders within the department. In the same way, it is also important to keep in mind the coherence of your subject from the perspective of your SLT, your team, the pupils in the school, their parents and the wider community. In other words, what is the core purpose of your subject as you see it, and how do all of these groups of people understand and 'live out' this core purpose?

A head of English must be a strong practitioner and set an example to the department in terms of subject knowledge and pedagogy. In doing so, you'll be in a much better position to create the kind of culture that will be an inspiring place in which to teach and learn. At its core, education is the most human of endeavours – perhaps no more so than in the subject of English – and it is important that English teams are places of compassion, rigour, challenge, debate and everything in between.

Becoming a head of department (and indeed stepping up to other kinds of leadership in an English team) may sound like a daunting idea for many people who may have picked up this book with a view to becoming a better English teacher, but time flies (especially in teaching!), and you may be surprised when one day you have a sudden urge to move up the career ladder. Of course, it may be part of your long-term plan from the outset. Either way, this chapter seeks to address the best ways to approach this next step.

Research and theory

In the NAHT's report on life as a middle leader, James Bowen (2019) begins his foreword by saying that middle leaders 'provide a vital bridge between senior leaders and the teaching staff, acting as both a filter and buffer'. The report is an interesting one, because it is one of relatively few insights and research into the mechanics of middle leadership – including the perceptions and ideas of middle leaders themselves.

One of the key observations and recommendations is around the formal training and time (or lack of) for middle leaders to enhance their skills. Indeed, in some cases (including those of you reading this), people are thrown into middle leadership because they have shown strong teaching skills or another set of skills or proficiencies. The newly reformed National Professional Qualifications (NPQs) do seek to offer more formal experiences in order to develop skills that will prepare you for middle leadership, and if offered by your school, these sorts of opportunities should be embraced with an open mind in terms of the learning experiences that they offer. Irrespective of all of this, there is nothing that will prepare you for that movement from unconscious incompetence to conscious incompetence and beyond – and that's OK.

As referenced in the report, there's a sense that the majority of middle leaders are held to high standards, but with a lack of time to really get to grips with the strategic, operational and emotional aspects of the role. You should recognise this, but use this knowledge and remember to be outward-looking as you make your initial steps into middle leadership.

As for personality, everyone is different and there is no expectation for you to be a certain way. Jamie Thom, in his book *A Quiet Education* (2020), includes a chapter on quiet leadership, with a reminder that we don't need to be extroverted. He uses the example of Neil Armstrong as a 'humble, eloquent hero' (Buzz Aldrin was initially meant to step onto the moon first). You may surprise yourself if you are not loud and are more likely to be successful if you are calm and measured. We can all think of leaders who are like a swan on the outside but are still paddling away invisibly yet furiously underneath – ultimately reliable and steadying. Indeed, the very title of John Tomsett and Jonny Uttley's book *Putting Staff First* (2020), more a book for SLT, yet still relevant at middle management level, is a reminder that the team is what counts. Being a head of department brings many day-to-day tasks, but you can't achieve anything without your team, and what they don't need is a bulldozer or someone who instils panic.

Thinking about and developing your interpersonal skills will help you on your journey to middle leadership (and even in your classroom practice). Mary Myatt writes about the importance of treating people as 'humans first, professionals second' in *Back on Track* (2020), pointing out that people are happier to be held to account when they are treated well. In this, she also references Kim Scott's ideas in *Radical Candor* (2019). Those tough decisions and difficult conversations won't go away, but will ultimately be easier as you build strong and productive relationships. Everyone wants to improve, and our role is to facilitate that, as well as looking to improve ourselves and build an environment where individuals are always actively seeking to improve.

Consider also the subheading of Mary Myatt's book, *Back on Track: Fewer things, greater depth* (2020); she has a clear focus on clearing the clutter. Is this something you can start to do at an earlier stage in your own day-to-day practice?

Putting it into practice

Preparing for promotion

There is no expected timeline for promotion; in fact, you don't have to be looking for a promotion at all if it doesn't suit you. There are plenty of incredible practitioners who have never felt the need to climb the ladder, or who have tried it and decided it isn't for them – indeed, where would we be without these kinds of experienced teachers? And different routes suit different characters – the head of department role is not the only way to go. What about lead practitioner roles, or maybe the pastoral route is for you? It takes all sorts to run a school. A good activity to try that may help you decide which role is best for you is to ask yourself: which elements of my role do I enjoy the most? You could also write a list of these elements and then see where they best fit in terms of a leadership position. You may well find that they are best suited to academic leadership, or it might be that they are best suited to the pastoral leadership structure.

When a member of your team announces that they want to move on, try asking two questions: firstly, are you bored? Secondly, are you unhappy? If the answer to either of these questions is 'yes', then a discussion needs to be had about how to put this right. If you've been paying attention to the needs of your team, you will hopefully already know the answer to these questions and will have intercepted any such feelings with possible solutions.

But these are also questions you should be asking yourself on a regular basis. Don't allow yourself to become bored or unhappy in your work. An observant head of department will be aware of your developmental needs and will push you on, even to the point of encouraging you to apply for promotions elsewhere if appropriate! Picture this scenario: a brilliant but shy colleague is encouraged to apply for a second-in-command role in another school – they get the job, become head of department soon after and never look back. Nobody wants them to leave and their experience is missed dreadfully, but sometimes members of your team outgrow their role and it is time for them to move on and develop further. True story!

Any journey to leadership will be unique, but finding the best opportunities to build your CV is key, and whatever they include, they should involve leading others. The making and sharing of resources – something you might do as a member of any departmental team – is not enough. Curriculum development (different from resource creation) is a key part of any departmental team working together; having that overview and understanding of *why* you are doing it is essential. Even more important is the way that you then communicate with the team, monitoring, reviewing and following up on the work you have put in place. Any responsibility you take on needs to have an element of team development and leadership, and this is the main difference between an interview for a teaching role and an interview for a leadership role. Leading and dealing with the different personalities in your team – the inexperienced, the non-specialists, those with wider-school teaching and learning responsibilities (TLRs), the keen and the reluctant – will prepare you for the day you are thrown in at the deep end with a team of your own.

Do also consider looking beyond your department for developmental opportunities – leading a small team on a school-wide project or being part of a working group are useful starting points. That said, do not let your school take advantage and give you huge, unpaid responsibilities that should carry a TLR!

During this time, you should also be starting to consider what kind of leader you want to be. Look around you: who do you admire most (and least)? Why? What do they do specifically that can make a difference to the way you want to lead others? What do you need to change or gain experience in, that will help you to become the leader you want to be? The worst might be disorganised and detached; the best might be great communicators and listeners, have had a clear vision and have seemed unflappable when their team members have needed it. There is a lot to be said about a leader who shows empathy.

Wider reading and an involvement in educational discussion are also ways in which you can prepare yourself for leadership. Develop your opinions on different aspects of education and engage in educational discussion on Twitter or other platforms; engage in CPD that involves, but also goes beyond, subject knowledge; read research papers and blogs... maybe even write some of your own and put yourself out there! We are so lucky that there are so many voices to expand and challenge our thinking, and we should take advantage of that. For handy hashtags to follow, try #TeamEnglish and #Litdrive. Just a few people to follow might include Jennifer Webb and Alex Quigley for English-specific content, and for wider curriculum information, Mary Myatt and Christine Counsell.

Taking the leap: applying for a head of department role

When you decide it is time to start making applications, be patient and focus on what you are looking for in a school, department or role. Finding the right school can make all the difference; you don't want to start your leadership experience in a poorly led school where you get little say in what changes can be made, where support is lacking, or where the ethos of the school is at odds with your own. Do your research – ask around, follow school leaders and teachers on Twitter, and ask to tour the school (always during the school day) before making an application.

When writing your letter, all of your experience needs to come into play. The focus is no longer wholly on your ability within the classroom, but now needs to look beyond it and have a clear focus on the skills and personalities which will help you to become not just a good manager, but a strong and effective leader. Use the skills, attributes and roles listed in the job description, but perhaps some of the most important things to be able to show are as follows:

- **Knowledge of the school:** Ensure as far as you can that your letter is tailored to the needs of the school you are applying to. Do not produce a generic head of department application letter that you paste into the application form every time you see a new post advertised. Show that you are already invested in the role.

- **Adaptability:** Prove that you are able to review and adapt to situations as necessary, recognising the need for change, but also accepting that you won't get it just right first time round.

- **Strong communication and listening skills:** Any strong leader will listen to their team as well as reading and discussing educational concepts. You won't always agree and make the changes they suggest, but the openness for discussion is key.

- **Mindset and vision:** Have a strategic mindset as well as an overarching vision for how you would lead the department.

- **Leading by example:** Show your enthusiasm, organisation, strong subject knowledge and pedagogical skill.

- **Empathy but also strength:** As a head of department, you should have the ability to motivate and support others when they need you, but also the ability to challenge, make difficult decisions, and recognise and accept when things go wrong. (This involves having the resilience and ability to find practical solutions to put things right.)

- **Teamwork:** The ability to be a part of, as well as the leader of, a team is crucial.

- **Humility:** Accept that you will also need support at times.

The interview

Having been offered the interview, you need to prepare effectively so that you can give it your all. There could be stiff competition: how serious a contender are you? And even if the competition isn't stiff, don't you just want them to think you are perfect for the job? (Remember, they don't have to appoint from this pool of candidates…) Go through the school details again: what is important to them? What are they likely to ask in the interview? Plan and rehearse answers for questions out loud, and ensure you can develop your answers with evidence. Be ready to demonstrate and evaluate the effectiveness of anything you say you have done and how you might have adapted your practice as a result. They won't expect perfection, but they will expect you to have the ability to be reflective and adaptable.

Here are some questions you could prepare for:

- Why is this the right point to apply for a TLR? And why this specific post or school?

- What are the qualities of an effective team leader?

- What is your departmental vision?

- How would you make the English department a stand-out department in the school?

- What would you aim to achieve in the first year and first three years?

- What do you think the challenges of this particular role might be? (Pick the two or three challenges you would be able to address.)

- How would you describe yourself in three words? Be prepared to back these up with specific examples.

- If you overheard some students or team members talking about you, what might they be saying?

- Describe a difficult piece of feedback you received – what was it, why was it difficult and what was the impact?

- How would you support and develop staff and what experience have you already had of this?

- What steps would you take to ensure your team is working to maximum impact?

- What makes good learning as opposed to good teaching?

- What makes a successful scheme of work and curriculum?

- How do you ensure consistency across a department?

- How would you use data to improve progress across the department?

- Outline what assessment strategies you would expect to see in the department.

- Scenario: A member of staff doesn't… How do you follow up with this? (This question might also ask for examples. Be prepared to be pushed beyond your initial answer, e.g. 'What if they still don't?'.)

- Scenario: You observe a lesson where… How do you deal with the situation? (This could be pupil- or teacher-related – or both!)

- Talk about a difficult situation when you did everything you could but things didn't turn out as you would have wished.

- Give an example of CPD you have led, or a change you have overseen, and explain its effectiveness.

- What kind of enrichment opportunities can you see your department offering?

- (In schools with a sixth form:) How do you propose to improve (or maintain) Key Stage 5 recruitment?

- (If the role includes responsibility for literacy:) How do you develop whole-school literacy?

In addition, an interview for such a role might involve participating in other activities to test your skill and potential as a leader. Tasks you might be expected to carry out could include the following (thanks to EduTwitter for sharing some of these!):

- In-tray tasks will expect you to prioritise and explain how you would deal with the varied tasks you might face upon arrival on a day when you are running late and need to print a resource you made last night for period 1 (and yes, some mornings are like this!). For example:

  ○ You have an email reminding you that the deadline to write a blurb for the Year 9 options booklet was yesterday.
  ○ An angry parent has emailed to make a complaint and says they are coming into school to see you before school starts (their child has an English lesson in period one).
  ○ A team member is upset.
  ○ A school governor has emailed to ask to visit the department.
  ○ A teacher has gone home sick and has not left cover work.
  ○ A staff member has raised a child protection concern after reading yesterday's classwork.

- Interview a student and decide their teaching group and predicted grade based on the conversation.

- Complete a data analysis task in which you identify underachievers and trends, then present on how you would address this.

- Critique an existing scheme of work or curriculum.

- Participate in a 'department meeting' for candidates – discuss the data profile of a year group and come up with strategies for development.

- Mark a sample of real Year 11 mock papers and create an action plan for revision of that unit.

- Give a presentation to the department on an evaluation of their curriculum map and what you would do to develop it further.

- Give a presentation on your vision and values, or your vision for your role as a middle leader.

To an extent, you will make your own luck by being fully prepared. However, do remember that they may be looking for a specific personality or 'fit' and if you are not appointed, then you just have to accept that this one wasn't for you and keep looking for the right school. You should also consider your own views on this front. It might be that you feel that this isn't actually the place for you; there is no shame in pulling out. A number of this book's authors have done this with no regrets. Trust your gut feelings. You may find yourself sitting through interviews and wondering why you feel uninterested – maybe this school isn't quite what you are looking for; actually going through with it is a waste of everyone's time if you really don't want the job. So think carefully while you are there: how do you really feel about this place and these people, and do you really want to commit to this particular establishment? If not, then walk away.

Building your team

Becoming a head of department in any situation is pretty daunting. Ideas, idealism, leadership books and all the rest of it are one thing, but actually going into the situation for real, and managing the people and curriculum day to day is quite another. Something you cannot escape is that the way you see yourself – and the way others see you – will shift in a way you will probably not have encountered before. And that's OK – it's most likely how it should be.

At times, it can feel as if all the theory and management books you come across are utterly irrelevant to the lived reality; it takes time to understand that the two aren't completely disconnected. That is because you have to make sense of that connection in your own unique way. Whether it be strategy, leading from the front, managing people, theory or something else, there will be elements that come to you more naturally than others. Any kind of leadership is based on relationships; achieving those positive and productive relationships can be done in a variety of ways.

In truth, then, it is the people in your team who will deliver your curriculum: an English department can only *ever* be as effective as the people who are in it. Yes, your own principles, ideals and initiatives are all important ways of establishing credibility, but that is not where it should end: in truth, they are only part of the story. Those things only work if they are part of the relationships that you forge with the people in your team as you begin to build it.

It might seem counterintuitive, but in many ways the best thing to do is probably *very little*. If you plough on with your own initiatives and ideas, you might make some small gains, but it's likely that patience and listening will provide you with the areas of development that will have the most meaningful impact. Maybe try making a list of all the things you are itching to introduce, then take a good look at whether they are, in truth, *your* personal preferences, whether there are existing systems that might achieve the same outcomes, and which ones are genuinely urgent and pressing.

When you eventually become a head of department, you will almost certainly inherit a range of experience, skills and motivations. It's vital to get to grips with this landscape as soon as you can. This way, when you begin to work out your priorities, when you do start to *do* stuff, it's less likely going to be wasted energy.

What exactly does all this mean, then? Taking the time to speak to your team collectively and individually is key. It's not controversial to begin simply by establishing an open culture of dialogue, ensuring that core resources are available for the coming weeks, and ensuring that the long-term plan (or at least the basic outline) is in place. From that point onwards, it establishes the conditions for other things to develop naturally. Lots of heads of department like to do experience and knowledge audits of their teams (reflecting both subject knowledge as well as areas linked with pedagogy) to get a real sense of what they have in the building to tap into for department CPD and indeed, areas that need developing in the team. An example is given opposite for English language (a literature version might link to particular texts, characters, themes and literary movements, for example).

Managing your team

Before we say anything else, it's really important to recognise that managing your team will very likely depend on a number of variables: the two most significant are whether you are stepping up from within your team (and your colleagues may have to get used to seeing you in a different way), or whether you are coming in as an outsider. Both have their challenges, but most people would probably say that the former is more difficult and more complex. Below, we will discuss and outline ways in which you can continually manage the tension between strategy and operation – if the job can be summed up in a phrase, it's probably that: the interplay between strategy and operation.

	Red Unconfident: would really benefit from CPD here	Amber Secure in my knowledge but would appreciate further CPD	Green Feel confident: an area of strength in my teaching
English language			
Language analysis			
Structural analysis			
Language evaluation			
Descriptive/ narrative writing			
Synthesis			
Comparing viewpoints			
Non-fiction writing to inform			
Non-fiction writing to argue			
Non-fiction writing to persuade			

Before starting with any of that, though, it's really important to give you some reference points to begin to understand the psychological aspect of the role. On a practical note, one thing a lot of people find useful is 'plotting' their team on a piece of paper. Yes, there is a touch of David Brent to this, but it's a sound thing to do in terms of visualising your own understanding of your team: it really forces you to unpick, frame and reframe where people in your team stand and feel in relation to each other. If you understand this, you will be in a much better place to understand and anticipate the pitfalls and implications of decisions that you may make. It's basically a case of drawing circles and seeing which circles overlap in terms of friendship and social groups, and it's surprisingly useful. Of course, there's nothing stopping you from revisiting it either.

The Johari window is also a very useful tool to invest some time in, if only for ten minutes or so. This model has four quadrants which ask you to think about your personality traits and decide which ones are:

1. known to yourself and known to others (open area or arena)

2. known to yourself but not known to others (hidden area or façade)

3. not known to yourself but known to others (blind spot)

4. not known to yourself and not known to others (unknown).

You can find an image of the model here: https://images.app.goo.gl/ou6s2ch1bmnQ1egX6. The Johari window is an extremely useful tool because it forces you to consider all facets of your identity in a wider context, including the things that others do and do not know about you. In essence, things that might be triggering your own behaviours that others might not be aware of.

Again, being self-reflective is vital. Lots of heads of department are continually struck by the emotionally overwhelming dimension of the job, and it is undoubtedly the case that the worst types of conflict occur when people begin to lack perspective and aren't able to grasp where others are coming from.

At its base, just like the above idea of sketching out the team's knowledge and experience, it's about understanding yourself – and how you see yourself – in relation to others. Take the time to do it – it's very powerful stuff of which to remain aware. Again, many heads of department find doing a 'staff voice' exceptionally useful in terms of things that have been useful and things that have been less useful in relation to workload and helping student progress. Again, this is one of those things that will help you to navigate between the theory/strategy and practice/operation axes.

It's a well-worn cliché now, but all of these things tap into the *why* of English teams. It's the head of department's job to establish the conditions for others to thrive. Humans thrive on consistency, certainty and predictability.

Simon Sinek (2011) has famously spoken of the importance of the 'why' in motivating people; in other words, a compelling vision and story for your curriculum underpinned by heartfelt values is crucial, but it can't end there. This is where it is crucial to have a decent range of teaching experience before becoming a middle leader – only then can you truly empathise and understand the implications of what you are asking your team to do.

You can provide consistency and predictability by ensuring that long-term plans are clearly established and shared, including unit starts and ends, school holidays, assessment and data points as a minimum. You can then share key dates on a weekly basis if that's something that people find useful. Also, in terms of quality assurance, place these on the long-term plans, and ask people with responsibility to protectively and positively run their areas and have real ownership of this process. Again, the theme of linking the short, medium and long term is seen when we start to consider sharing your 'team

Improvement priority	Success criteria	R	A	G
We achieve better than the national average for both language and literature (positive residual).	With particular focus on Year 11, you've taken action to identify gaps in knowledge; you are aware of where the gaps in skills and knowledge are and what you are going to do to rectify this.			
	You are aware of underperforming cohorts, and who the individuals are in your own classes (including seating plans and class lists) – pupil premium; boys; also sheets that head of department provides after data trawl.			
Our results for writing in GCSE language are higher than 'similar centres' (AQA Enhanced Results Analysis will tell us this).	You give all of your classes extended periods of writing time, especially non-fiction and fiction writing pieces.			
	Your classes are exposed to a range of quality fiction or non-fiction writing every lesson.			
	You are aware of the fiction and non-fiction writing resources in One Drive, and have reflected upon how you may use them in your own lessons.			

We ensure productive use of feedback in all lessons.	You ensure pupils benefit from purple-pen time in order to improve their work, and pupils also use green pen to peer assess as well as reflecting upon their own work. Purple-pen tasks are diagnostic and give pupils the chance to focus on a particular aspect of their work.
Books are consistently of a high standard.	You relentlessly challenge poor or careless work in books; you use the redraft/redo and underline date/title stamp. You ask pupils to repeat work when it is not of an acceptable standard (at home if necessary).
We establish a clear framework for pupils to become independent learners, especially in the event of pupils not being able to be present in school.	All of your classes have access to Bedrock (if appropriate), Educake, Seneca, Showbie. You set all homework on Showbie so that it can be used as a medium of communication should the need arise.
We continue to provide an enriching English curriculum outside of the classroom.	You are aware of the extra curricular activities that the department provides for pupils, and are able to recommend these to pupils where appropriate.

	2018	2019	2020	2021
	Pupil premium scores in brackets			
7+				
5+				
4+				
P8				

priorities' and what this actually looks like day to day. Your team can again RAG-rate themselves against these areas, and have a real understanding of how they are contributing to the overall vision and success of the team. See pages 230–2 for an example.

Things like schemes of learning and units of work need to have a consistent look and feel too – this reduces mental strain when accessing resources, again giving colleagues more time and space to focus on what matters. In simple terms, this cuts to the chase when your team begins to teach a sequence of lessons: they should know the content and skills being taught on a week-by-week basis. Once this is in place, teachers can really begin to get on with the business of adapting this framework for their students in a way that best suits them.

It's really important to establish this stuff, as it makes the business of managing people more straightforward: if everything is in place and agreed upon, it makes supposedly 'difficult conversations' much less complex. The very worst environments are often ones where clarity is simply not forthcoming, no one knows whether they are coming or going, and everyone spends more time worrying about what they aren't doing rather than proactively taking a clear outline and structure and making it meaningful for their own classrooms.

One thing that's touched on above is the link between strategy and operations: depending on the size of your team, although the number and range of responsibilities will vary between teams, one thing that's universal is that the relationship between the head of department and TLR holders is essential to make sure that your department 'walks the walk'. Again, whether you call it 'the why', 'the vision' or 'the ethos', there should be a really consistent feel about the priorities and what your team is trying to achieve at any one moment. This might be one or a number of the following:

- a specific teaching and learning focus

- a focus on a cohort of pupils

- a focus on an area of the curriculum

- a particular focus on something linked with the 'whole-school' context.

Within this, communication is obviously key. While not going into too much depth, streamlining is important here, as well as thinking about the timings of emails. Most email now has the ingenious option of 'sending later'. If an email can wait until the following morning, delay it so people aren't going to spend their evenings or holidays on this. There is also something appalling about the ominous email asking a colleague to 'come and see you' tomorrow without any sense of what this is linked with. It's unnecessary. Many of us have been on the receiving end of these things, and they are – at worst – an appalling powerplay, and at best, unthinking: so don't do it! Again, in terms of communications, this is more about access to crucial information than anything else (assessments and dates, quality assurance calendar and so forth), with any crucial variations in a place that *isn't* just an email that will have to be searched for later. Apps like Microsoft Teams and Google Meetings are useful platforms, but there are lots of e-noticeboards that are free and available to use if you search around (Padlet is great).

Developing your team

Another thing to consider is that it's important to continually look to develop people around you. We have a responsibility to move people on. It's really healthy to talk in terms of the 'ecosystems of schools'; in essence, it *shouldn't* matter if we develop someone who moves on somewhere else and is successful – we need to get away from this line of thinking that we schools are individual silos operating in a way that others cannot and should not be impacted by. For you, this might mean completing an audit of the skills and confidence of the team in different areas of your curriculum and exam specification. You might have some hidden gems in your team, such as exam markers, or simply people who have life experiences that can be harnessed for the betterment of colleagues and students. We live in a world of social media that enables us to network and bring skills in from other schools; people are always looking for the opportunity to give themselves new experiences of leadership – why not ask them to present to your team?

Again, empowering people and letting them know that you have one eye on their development is another way of delegating and managing your own workload. It has been known for heads of department to take advantage of teachers wanting to progress. Do be sure that you are not offering 'development opportunities' because you don't want to do something; be comfortable that what you are offering is providing opportunities to aid progression. Depending on the size of your team, you might find it useful to give people mini-projects for curriculum development, or to put together a department CPD timetable for a 20-minute input from someone on a particular aspect of teaching or subject knowledge. Just like consistency and predictability, it's natural to want to feel like you are contributing and you are a valued member of the team. If you see something to celebrate, then do it. Schools are often terrible places for not showing appreciation for brilliant things: you can change that in your own team.

Just as teaching itself is about having a clear sense of purpose and identity, this is the case when it comes to leading from the middle as well. Above all else, the most inspirational middle leaders are the ones who are values driven; this is hardly surprising, but the most important thing is for you to reflect on what those values are. Once you have reflected upon this, you will undoubtedly be in a much better position to demonstrate and use all of the fantastic skills and qualities that you will have no doubt demonstrated in order to find yourself in the position of a middle leader in the first place.

Summary

- Build your brand: what do you stand for? How do you see yourself in your chosen leadership role? How will you ensure you will be the leader you want to be?
- Prepare yourself: what will your pathway be in preparation for leadership? What do you need experience of and how will you ensure you get it?
- Know your vision: what is your philosophy? What, ultimately, is essential for your pupils, team and school?
- Know your stuff, both subject specific and pedagogy. Be curious, discuss pedagogy and have opinions.
- Use and develop your team to your (and their) best advantage. Value their strengths, develop their weaknesses and allow them the best opportunities you can.
- Lead by example: don't ask your team to do anything you aren't already doing (and doing well!) or are prepared to do.

References

Adichie, C. N. (2009), 'The danger of a single story', www.ted.com/talks/chimamanda_ngozi_adichie_the_danger_of_ a_single_story

Alexander, R. J. (2004), *Towards Dialogic Teaching: Rethinking Classroom Talk*. Dialogos.

AQA (2019), 'GCSE English Language 8700/2 Paper 2: Report on the Examination', https://filestore.aqa.org.uk/sample-papers-and-mark-schemes/2019/june/AQA-87002-WRE-JUN19.PDF

Ashmore, J. and Clay, C. (2016), *The New Middle Leader's Handbook*. Woodbridge: John Catt.

Bambrick-Santoyo, P. (2016), *Get Better Faster*. San Francisco, CA: Jossey Bass.

Beck. I., McKeown, M. G. and Kucan, L. (2013), *Bringing Words to Life* (2nd edn.). London: The Guilford Press.

Berger, R. (2003), *An Ethic of Excellence: Building a Culture of Craftsmanship with Students*. Portsmouth, NH: Heinemann Educational Books.

Bjork, R. A. (1988), 'Retrieval practice and the maintenance of knowledge', in M. M. Gruneberg, P. E. Morris and R. N. Sykes (eds.), *Practical Aspects of Memory II*. London: Wiley.

Bjork, R.A. (1994), 'Memory and metamemory considerations in the training of human beings', in J. Metcalfe and A. Shimamura (eds.), *Metacognition: Knowing about knowing*. Cambridge, MA: MIT Press.

Bjork, E.L. and Bjork, R.A. (2009), 'Making Things Hard on Yourself, But in a Good Way: Creating Desirable Difficulties to Enhance Learning', in M. A. Gernsbacher, L.M. Hough, R. W. Pew and J.R. Pomerantz (eds.), *Psychology and the Real World: Essays Illustrating Fundamental Contributions to Society*. Gordonsville, VA: Worth Publishers.

Booker, C. (2004), *The Seven Basic Plots: Why we tell stories*. London: Continuum.

Borko, H., Livingston, C. and Shavelson, R. J. (1990), 'Teachers' thinking about instruction', *Remedial and Special Education*, 11, (6), 40–49.

Caviglioli, O. and Sherrington, T. (date unknown), '9 evidence-based feedback techniques for secondary school poster', www.teachwire.net/teaching-resources/9-evidence-based-feedback-techniques-for-secondary-school-poster

Christodoulou, D. (2017a), 'Teaching knowledge or teaching to the test?', https://daisychristodoulou.com/2017/01/teaching-knowledge-or-teaching-to-the-test

Christodoulou, D. (2017b), *Making Good Progress?* Oxford: Oxford University Press.

Clark, C., Picton, I. and Lant, F. (2020), 'National Literacy Trust research report: "More time on my hands": Children and young people's writing during the COVID-19 lockdown in 2020', https://cdn.literacytrust.org.uk/media/documents/Writing_during_the_COVID-19_lockdown_report.pdf

Counsell, C. (2018), 'Senior curriculum leadership 1: the indirect manifestation of knowledge: (B) final performance as deceiver and guide', https://thedignityofthethingblog.wordpress.com

Cowan, N. (2010), 'The Magical Mystery Four: How Is Working Memory Capacity Limited, and Why?', *Current Directions in Psychological Science*, 19, 51–57 .

Crystal, D. (2005), *The Stories of English*. London: Penguin.

Crystal, D. (2007), *Words Words Words*. Oxford: Oxford University Press.

Curtis, C. (2019), *How to Teach: English*. Carmarthen: Crown House.

Department for Education (2012), 'What is the research evidence on writing?', www.gov.uk/government/publications/what-is-the-research-evidence-on-writing

Department for Education (2013), 'National curriculum in England: secondary curriculum', www.gov.uk/government/publications/national-curriculum-in-england-secondary-curriculum

Department for Education (2018), 'School workforce in England: November 2017', www.gov.uk/government/statistics/school-workforce-in-england-november-2017

Department for Education (2019), 'Teacher workload survey 2019', www.gov.uk/government/publications/teacher-workload-survey-2019

Didau, D. (2014), 'The glamour of grammar: in context or not?', https://learningspy.co.uk/english-gcse/glamour-grammar

EEF (2019a), 'Grammar for Writing (re-grant)', https://educationendowmentfoundation.org.uk/projects-and-evaluation/projects/grammar-for-writing-effectiveness-trial

EEF (2019b), 'Improving literacy in secondary schools', https://educationendowmentfoundation.org.uk/toolsguidance-reports/improving-literacy-in-secondary-schools/

EEF (2020), 'Metacognition and self-regulated learning', https://educationendowmentfoundation.org.uk/tools/guidance-reports/metacognition-and-self-regulated-learning

Enow, L. and Goodwyn, A. (2017), 'Multimethod study: Secondary English teacher cognition', *SAGE Research Methods Cases Part 2*. London: SAGE.

Enow, L. and Goodwyn, A. (2018), 'The invisible plan: how English teachers develop their expertise and the special place of adapting the skills of lesson planning', *English in Education*, 52, (2), 120–134.

Ericsson, A. and Pool, R. (2016), *Peak: Secrets from the New Science of Expertise*. London: Bodley Head.

Facer, J. (2013), 'In praise of re-reading', https://readingallthebooks.com/2013/07/20/in-praise-of-re-reading

Freytag, G. (1894), *Freytag's Technique of the Drama: An exposition of dramatic composition and art*.

Hill, C. and Howard, K. (2020) *Symbiosis: The Curriculum and the Classroom*. Woodbridge: John Catt.

Hiscock, A. and Wilcox, H. (2017), *The Oxford Handbook of Early Modern English Literature and Religion*. Oxford: Oxford University Press.

Hochman, J. C. (2017), *The Writing Revolution*. San Francisco, CA: Jossey Bass.

Jones, S., Myhill, D. A. and Bailey T. (2012), 'Grammar for writing? An investigation of the effects of contextualised grammar teaching on students' writing', *Reading and Writing*, 26, (8).

Kara, B. (2020), *A Little Guide for Teachers: Diversity in Schools*. London: Corwin.

Kispal, A. (2007), 'Effective teaching of inference skills for reading', www.nfer.ac.uk/publications/edr01/edr01.pdf

Kirsch, I., de Jong, J., Lafontaine, D., McQueen, J., Mendelovits, J., & Monseur, C. (2002), *Reading for change: Performance and engagement across countries: Results from PISA 2000*. Paris, France: Organization for Economic Co-operation and Development (OECD).

Land, R., Cousin, G., Meyer, J. H. F. and Davies, P. (2005), 'Threshold concepts and troublesome knowledge (3): Implications for course design and evaluation', in C. Rust (ed.), *Improving Student Learning – equality and diversity*. Oxford: OCSLD.

Langacker, R. (1987), *Foundations of Cognitive Grammar (Vol. I)*. Stanford, CA: Stanford University Press.

Lemov, D. (2015), *Teach Like a Champion* 2.0. San Francisco, CA: Jossey-Bass.

Lemov, D., Driggs, C. and Woolway, E. (2016), *Reading Reconsidered*. San Francisco, CA: Jossey Bass.

Low, G. and Wynne-Davies, M. (2006), *A Black British Canon?* Basingstoke: Palgrave Macmillan.

Maybank, D. (2018), 'An introduction to Restoration comedy', www.bl.uk/restoration-18th-century-literature/articles/an-introduction-to-restoration-comedy

Meally, M. and Bowen, N. (2015), *The Art of Writing English Literature Essays*. Peripeteia Press.

Myatt, M. (2020), *Back on Track*. Woodbridge: John Catt.

Myhill, D. (2014), 'Foreword', in E. Curran and H. Lines (eds.), *KS3 Skills for Writing*. London: Pearson.

National Center for Education Statistics. (2013), *The nation's report card: Trends in academic progress 2012 (NCES 2013 456)*. Washington, DC: U.S. Department of Education Institute of Education Sciences.

NFER (2020), 'Teacher Labour Market in England Annual Report 2020', www.nfer.ac.uk/teacher-labour-market-in-england-annual-report-2020

Nuthall, G. (2007), *The Hidden Lives of Learners*. Wellington: NZCER Press.

Ofsted (2019), 'Education inspection framework', www.gov.uk/government/publications/education-inspection-framework

Perkins, D. (1992), *Smart Schools: Better Thinking and Learning for Every Child*. New York: Free Press.

Pryke, S. and Staniforth, A. (2020), *Ready to Teach: Macbeth*. Woodbridge: John Catt.

Quigley, A. (2018), *Closing the Vocabulary Gap*. Abingdon: Routledge.

Quigley, A. (2020), *Closing the Reading Gap*. Abingdon: Routledge.

Read On, Get On (2015), 'Ready to read: closing the gap in early language skills so that every child in England can read well'. London: Save the Children.

Renaissance Learning. (2015), *The research foundation for Accelerated Reader 360*. Wisconsin Rapids, WI: Author.

Rosenshine, B. (2012), 'Principles of instruction: research-based strategies that all teachers should know', *American Educator*, 36, 12–19.

Rowlands, L. and Riley, K. (2021), 'A bookletised curriculum', https://hodandheart.co.uk/product/a-bookletised-curriculum-with-laura-rowlands-and-kaley-riley/

Scott, K. (2019), *Radical Candor*. London: Pan Macmillan.

Sherrington, T. and Caviglioli, O. (2020), *Teaching Walk-Thrus: Five-Step Guides to Instructional Coaching*. Woodbridge: John Catt.

Shimamura, A. (2018), *MARGE*. Self-published.

Sinek, S. (2011), *Start With Why*. London: Penguin.

Storr, W. (2019), *The Science of Storytelling*. London: HarperCollins.

Sumeracki, M. (2020), 'Elaboration as Self-explanation', www.learningscientists.org/blog/2020/2/20-1

Sutherland, J. (2013), *A Little History of Literature*. London: Yale University Press.

Sweller, J., van Merrienboer, J. J. G. and Paas, F. G. W. C. (1998), 'Cognitive architecture and instructional design', *Educational Psychology Review*, 10, 251–296

Thom, J. (2020), *A Quiet Education*. Woodbridge: John Catt.

Tomsett, J. and Uttley, J. (2020), *Putting Staff First*. Woodbridge: John Catt.

Webb, J. (2019), *How to Teach English Literature*. Woodbridge: John Catt.

Wellcome Trust (2018), 'Developing great subject teaching', https://wellcome.org/sites/default/files/developing-great-subject-teaching.pdf

Wiliam, D. (2013), *Example of really big mistake: calling formative assessment formative assessment rather than something like "responsive teaching"* [Twitter.] 23 October, https://twitter.com/dylanwiliam/status/393045049337847808

Wiliam, D. (2014), 'Principled assessment design', https://webcontent.ssatuk.co.uk/wp-content/uploads/2013/09/RS8-Principled-assessment-design-chapter-one.pdf

Wiliam, D. (2016), 'The nine things every teacher should know', www.tes.com/news/dylan-wiliam-nine-things-every-teacher-should-know

Wiliam, D. (2017), *I've come to the conclusion Sweller's Cognitive Load Theory is the single most important thing for teachers to know http://bit.ly/2kouLOq.* [Twitter.] 26 January, https://twitter.com/dylanwiliam/status/824682504602943489

Wiliam, D. (2019), 'Teaching not a research-based profession', www.tes.com/news/dylan-wiliam-teaching-not-research-based-profession

Willingham, D. T. (2009), *Why Don't Students Like School?* San Francisco, CA: Jossey Bass.

Willingham, D. T. (2014), 'Strategies that make learning last', *Educational Leadership*, 72, (2), 10–15.

Willingham, D. T. and Lovette, G. (2014), 'Can reading comprehension be taught?', *Teachers College Record.* www.danielwillingham.com/uploads/5/0/0/7/5007325/willingham&lovette_2014_can_reading_comprehension_be_taught_.pdf

Yorke, J. (2014), *Into the Woods*. London: Penguin.

Young, M. and Muller, J. (2013), 'On the powers of powerful knowledge', *Review of Education*, 1, 229–250.

Index

academic essay writing 108–11
additional responsibility 26–7
ancient Greek and earlier
	literature 82–4
Anglo-Saxon literature 84
assessments
	formative 54, 73–6
	GCSE-style 52–3
	meaning of 52–4
	Ofsted framework 53–4
	purpose of 54
	summative 54, 74, 76–7
	and validation 54

behaviour management 18–19
	objectivity 20
	positivity 19–20
	presence 20–1
blogs 125
box method, in writing 122–3
British Library 37, 91

Celtic literature 84
chanting 208–10
Chartered College of Teaching 171
children's literature 97–8
classic reads 147
classroom, reading in 148
	drama texts 140–1
	exam questions 151–3
	reading ages 149–50
	reciprocal reading 148–9, 180
cognitive load theory 176–8
cold reading 132–9
communication 233–4

comparison of writing 112–14
comprehension 128, see also
	reading
concepts 59–60
constructs 59-60
continuing professional
		development (CPD) 13,
		24–26, 35, 37
	ECT 24–6
	sources for 37–8
		British Library 37
		department
			knowledge 39–40
		JSTOR 37–8
		online sources 38–9
		subject communities 40–1
		university libraries 38
core knowledge 56
curriculum planning
	conceptual development 59–60
		inference, implication and
			ambiguity 63–4
		literary allusion and
			intertextuality 62–3
		motif and trope 62
		narrative voice and
			perspective 61
		plot 61–2
		reading narrative 60–1
	core knowledge for 55–6
	disciplinary knowledge for 57
	lesson planning 71–2
	long-term planning 64–5
	medium-term planning 65–70
	powerful knowledge for 55–8

procedural knowledge for 57
substantive knowledge for 56
threshold concepts for 56–7, 60
and vision 55

deep content exploration 180
descriptive writing 122–3
disciplinary knowledge 57
disciplinary literacy 164
drama texts 139
  in classroom 140–1
  rhythm and rhyme 141
  stage production 139–40
dual coding 184–6

Early Career Framework (ECF) 6,
  8–9, 11
early career teacher (ECT) 5
  behaviour management 18–19
    objectivity 20
    positivity 19–20
    presence 20–1
  building support networks
    during 8–9
    academic teams 10
    non-teaching staff 11
    pastoral teams 10–11
    teaching team 9–10
  and career progression 26–7
  continuing professional
    development (CPD) 13, 24–6
  feedback 21
    asking for actions 22–3
    breaking targets into granular
      action steps 23
    concreteness of 21
    follow-up 24
    responding to 24
    understanding focus areas
      from 22
  maintaining balance 15
    exercise 16
    hobbies and interests 15
    loving the subject 15

staying connected with
  people 16
mentor of 11–13
retention of 6
skills development 16
  feedback versus marking 18
  planning 16–17
  teaching skills 17–18
structured programme for 6–7
time management 13
  diary 14
  owning space 14
  resource sites usage 14–15
early modern literature 87–9
Education Endowment Foundation
  (EEF) 6–7, 171, 179
effective argument, in
  writing 118–20
eighteenth century literature 91–2
elaboration, effective 202–3
  brain dump 203
  connecting ideas on same
    topic 204–5
  questioning 203–4
  retrieval of previously taught
    content 205–7
essay plans 207–8
exam questions 151–3
exercise 16
extrinsic motivation 182

fast reading 167–8
feedback
  for marginal gains 193–7
  versus marking 18
first year of teaching 5
forgetting, and learning 174–5
formative assessments 54, 73–6
4 As method, of writing 107
Freytag's model 34, 61, 159–60

Gothic literature 93
grammar 103
Gresham lectures 38

head of department 213–14
  application 219–20
  interpersonal skills
    development 216
  job interview 220–4
  NAHT's report 214–15
  personality uniqueness 215
  preparation for becoming 216–19
  team building 224–6
  team development 234–5
  team management 226–34
hinterland learning 55–6

inference 128–31
interleaving 188–9
intertextuality 62–3
intrinsic motivation 182
introduction writing 109
ITT Core Content Framework
  6–7, 8, 11

knowledge organisers 55, 183–
  4, 200–1

learning
  as change in long-term
    memory 175
  cognitive load theory 176–8
  cognitive science 71, 162–3
  dual coding 184–6
  feedback for marginal gains 193–7
  and forgetting 174–5
  hinterland learning 55–6
  interleaving and spacing 188–9
  knowledge organisers 183–4
  live modelling 186–8
  and memory 172
  metacognition 178–9
    thinking alone 179
    thinking aloud 181
    thinking efficiently 180–1
    thinking hard 181–2
    thinking positively 182
    thinking together 179–80

retrieval practice 184, 190–1
  and schema building 172–4
  walking talking mocks 191–3
  and working memory 175–6
lesson planning 71–2
library time 165–7
Litdrive UK 39
literature 79–81
  ancient Greek 82–83
    drama 83
    myths 82–3
    rhetoric 83
  Anglo-Saxon and Norse 84–5
  children's literature 97–8
  early modern and the
    Renaissance 87–9
  eighteenth century 91–2
  Middle English and
    medieval 85–7
  nineteenth century 92–4
  play texts 99–100
  reflections in current
    curriculum 81–2
  seminal world literature 96
  seventeenth century and the
    Restoration 89–91
  significance of 80
  twentieth century 94–6
live modelling, for learning 186–8

mapping vocabulary across
    curriculum 158, 162–4
marking versus feedback 18
memory, and learning 172
mentors 11–13
metacognition, of learning 178–9
  thinking alone 179
  thinking aloud 181
  thinking efficiently 180–1
  thinking hard 181–2
  thinking positively 182
  thinking together 179–80
Middle English and medieval
    literature 85–7

mind maps, complex 201–2
motif and trope 62

narrative voice and
       perspective 59, 61
narrative writing 120–1
National Professional Qualifications
       (NPQs) 215
nineteenth century literature 92–4
non-exam assessment (NEA) 44
    critical perspectives 48–9
    critical reading 47–8
    literature review 47–8
    planning out sections 47
    questions creation 46–7
    texts comparison 44–6
non-fiction writing 116–18
Norse literature 84
novice stage of teaching 7–8

organisation activity 180

pastoral teams 10–11
physical fitness 16
planning
    curriculum planning, see
       curriculum planning
    in ECT 16–17
play texts 99–100
post-colonial literature 95
post-war literature 95
powerful knowledge 55–8, 183
powerful openings, in
       writing 114–15
powerful sentences 106–8
principles of instruction 71–2
procedural knowledge 57
prompts 81, 191, 202, 203

qualified teacher status 5
questioning 203–4

reading 127
    in classroom 148

exam questions 151–3
    reading ages 149–50
    reciprocal reading 148–9, 180
drama texts 139
    in classroom 140–1
    rhythm and rhyme 141
    stage production 139–40
EEF recommendations
       148–9
EEF report 128
fast reading 167–8
inference 128–31
literary approach to texts
       131
    cold reading 132–9
    outset 131–2
for pleasure 145–6
    challenging concepts 147
    classic reads 147
    comfort reads 147
pre-1914 texts 142–3
reading narrative 60–1
reciprocal reading 148, 180
    clarifications 149
    prediction 148
    prior knowledge activation 148
    questioning 149
    summarising 149
relationship building 8–9, 10
Renaissance literature 87–9
resource sites 14–15
Restoration literature 89–91
retrieval practice 184, 190–1, 205–7
revision 199
    chanting 208–10
    complex mind maps 201–2
    effective elaboration 202–3
       brain dump 203
       connecting ideas on same
          topic 204–5
       questioning 203–4
       retrieval of previously taught
          content 205–7
    essay plans 207–8

knowledge organisers 200–1
rhetoric writing 118–20

schema building, for learning 172–4
SEEC model, for vocabulary 168–9
self-motivation 182
seminal world literature 96
seventeenth century
    literature 89–91
silent reading 165–7
spacing work, as learning
    method 189
strategy wall 180–1
'strong voice' technique 20
struggling readers 143–4
    modelling good reading
        behaviours 144
    pre-discussions 144–5
    re-reading 145
    summarising before
        beginning 144
subject knowledge 29–30
    A level
        non-exam assessment,
            see non-exam
            assessment (NEA)
        transition from GCSE to 43–4
        uptake of 42
    and big questions/enquiry
        questions 34–5
    case study 35–7
    and contextualisation 32–3
    CPD, see continuing
        professional
        development (CPD)
    and researching 30–1
subject-knowledge audit (SKA) 40
substantive knowledge 56
summative assessments 57,
    74, 76–7
support networks 8–11

TeachMeet 40–41
threshold concepts 56–7, 60

T.M.C. model, for writing 117–18
twentieth century literature 94–6

vocabulary 155–6
    development of 157–8
        building blocks 159
        colloquialisms 160–1
        Frayer model 159–60
    EEF report 156–7
    explicit instruction for 168–9
    form time 164–5
        fast reading 167–8
        silent reading and library
            time 165–7
        word of the week 165
    long-term planning 162–4
    tiered vocabulary 161–2

whole-class feedback 75–6
word of the week activity 165
working memory, and
    learning 175–6
working space 10
writing 101–2
    abstracts 123–4
    academic essay writing 108–11
    and connecting with
        people 124–5
    Department for Education
        report 102–3
    descriptive writing 122–3
    and grammar 103
    narrative writing 120–1
    National Literacy Trust
        report 102
    for newsletter, blog or vlog 125
    non-fiction 116–18
    powerful openings 114–16
    powerful sentences 106–8
    rhetoric or effective
        argument 118–20
    T.M.C. model 117–18
    word classes 103–6
    writing comparisons 112–14

Authors' biographies

Abigail Mann is an experienced teacher and currently works as an assistant headteacher as a school in Nottinghamshire. She leads on teaching and learning as well as curriculum and she is determined to level the playing field for the students she serves. As an advocate of the #Teacher5ADay initiative, she takes an active role in improving the wellbeing of teachers and students in schools across the country. She holds a genuine belief that the most successful schools are those in which staff and students' wellbeing is regarded as vital to their success, and has written two books on the subject: *Live Well, Teach Well* and *Live Well, Learn Well.* Follow Abigail on Twitter @abbiemann1982.

Fe Brewer has been enthusiastically teaching English in the East Midlands for over a decade; she also works in ITT as lead teacher educator for a SCITT, a role she is deeply passionate about after working as a subject specialism expert and a PGCE mentor for several years. Fe is also an evidence lead in education and a Litdrive regional advocate: two roles which allow her to share both her love of literature and educational research with other teachers. Fe is a keen presenter, having spoken at TeachMeets and conferences, including Team English and WomenEd, and has a reputation for her passionate delivery and flame-red hair. She tweets @mrsbrewtandcake.

Laura May Rowlands is proud to be head of English at Woodlands Community College in Southampton. She is a keen advocate for a sensible work-life balance in teaching. Outside of school life, she is kept busy with her two small sons, contributing articles to TES and volunteering for the charity #MTPTproject. She tweets about education, family life and work-life balance @tillyteacher.

Kaley Macis-Riley currently holds the role of head of English and whole school literacy lead at a school in Derbyshire, having taught for almost a decade. She runs her own education consultancy, HoDandHeart, providing CPD for teachers and school leaders. Kaley is incredibly passionate about using curriculum and pedagogy as a way to challenge social injustice, as well as the importance of ethical leadership and staff wellbeing, all of which she writes about often via her own blog and for TES. Kaley is studying for a master's degree in expert teaching and is a senior examiner. She tweets as @HoDandHeart.

Mary Hind-Portley is a highly experienced teacher and leader, having worked in a number of schools as a teacher, lead practitioner assistant head and curriculum director. In addition, Mary has also worked in a number of local authority school improvement roles. Mary is particularly focused on improving the progress and achievement of students who experience disadvantage through high quality curriculum planning and collaborative working practices. She is also a regional advocate (Merseyside) and blog curator for LitdriveUK. Mary is also a freelance writer and education blogger (https://hind-sights.com)and tweets as @Lit_Liverbird.

Ruth Holder is head of English at Priory C of E School in Dorking, where she also oversees leadership of the whole-school research hubs. Nearly 20 years of middle leadership experience have been spent working as a head of department, as well as supporting and leading a variety of whole-school projects. Her involvement in writing *Succeeding as an English Teacher* fulfils a childhood dream to be a writer. She is a Litdrive regional advocate and tweets @MrsRHEnglish.

Laura Tsabet is associate assistant principal of CPD and ITT across two secondary academies in Bournemouth. She has previously worked as director of initial teacher training, lead practitioner for teaching and learning, and assistant head of English. In addition to teaching, she has written regular columns for the *Times Educational Supplement*, acted as regional advocate for Litdrive for Dorset and the New Forest, and worked as a GCSE English literature examiner for a number of years. Laura is a firm believer in lifelong learning. She is currently studying for an NPQSL and plans to study for a master's degree in the near future. She tweets @lauratsabet.

Zara Shah has a master's degree in teaching and works as a Key Stage 3 English coordinator. She is a passionate advocate for research-informed pedagogy and has conducted a series of action research projects and case studies on the gender gap, metacognition and student learning behaviours. Zara regularly speaks at conferences such as Team English and WomenEd, and has co-organised TLLeeds. Zara is also an A level language examiner, a Litdrive regional advocate, a supporter of @EngchatUk and a co-opted governor at an outstanding primary school, working in collaboration with a family of local schools. as well as schools abroad. She is driven to ensure quality education for all. Follow Zara on Twitter @zssnas.

Holly Wimbush is head of KS4 Literature and subject leader of A Level Language and Literature at a secondary school in leafy Cheshire. After working as a subject mentor for five years, she is continuing to develop the next generation of teachers as a professional mentor. Holly firmly believes that curriculum is the key to providing powerful knowledge that will enable and empower all learners to master the challenges of today and shape the world of tomorrow. She has also led a number of whole-school CPD sessions ranging from effective RM+F to BfL across the school as well as leading content-based sessions for the faculty. Holly is a Litdrive regional advocate and also the regional networks associate. She tweets @HWimbushEnglish.

Lyndsay Bawden has been teaching English for over 20 years and in that time has held many roles, such as head of English and lead practitioner. She is a senior examiner for GCSE English Literature and a specialist leader in education. Lyndsay speaks at events such as the Schools and Academies Show, Team English Icons and WomenEd. She currently works as trust-wide English lead for the David Ross Education Trust, overseeing English in 11 secondary schools, and for Ark English Mastery as a school development lead, whilst also completing her master's degree in senior educational leadership. Lyndsay tweets @LyndsayBawden.

Davina Canham has taught for almost 20 years, both in the UK and abroad. Following her role as lead practitioner, she is now head of English at a secondary school in Northamptonshire. Davina is passionate about subject knowledge and has an master's degree in twentieth-century literature and its contexts. She is also passionate about developing subject-level CPD and has presented at Educating Northants, United Learning's English teacher conference and for Litdrive's remote CPD. As communications officer for Litdrive, Davina oversees all social media channels and the blog platform, and is the human being at the end of member updates and newsletters. Follow Davina on Twitter @DeeCanEnglish.

Andy Sammons is director of English at a large comprehensive school in Yorkshire. He has worked in schools for over ten years in roles including classroom teacher, lead practitioner and key stage leader. He is passionate about middle leadership and bringing out the best in others, and he has taken great pride in constructing a curriculum that is challenging, engaging and allows young people to understand the world around them. He is currently studying for a senior leader master's degree. Follow Andy on Twitter @andy_samm.